ROCK-BOTTOM BLESSINGS

ROCK-BOTTOM BLESSINGS

Discovering God's Abundance
When All Seems Lost

KAREN BEATTIE

LOYOLA PRESS.
A JESUIT MINISTRY
Chicago

LOYOLAPRESS.
A JESUIT MINISTRY

3441 N. Ashland Avenue
Chicago, Illinois 60657
(800) 621-1008
www.loyolapress.com

Some names in this book have been changed to protect privacy.

"The Touch" from THE COMPLETE POEMS by Anne Sexton, edited by Maxine Kumin.
© 1981 by Linda Gray Sexton and Loring Conant, Jr. Reprinted by permission of Houghton
Mifflin Harcourt Publishing Company. All rights reserved.

Cover art credit: Alloy Photography/Veer

Library of Congress Cataloging-in-Publication Data
Beattie, Karen.
   Rock-bottom blessings : discovering God's abundance when all seems lost / Karen Beattie.
      p. cm.
   ISBN-13: 978-0-8294-3842-0
   ISBN-10: 0-8294-3842-4
1. Beattie, Karen. 2. Christian biography—United States. I. Title.
   BR1725.B3875.A3 2013
   282.092—dc23
   [B]
                                                                    2012038747

Printed in the United States of America.
13 14 15 16 17 18 Bang 10 9 8 7 6 5 4 3 2 1

For David and Desta

Contents

God is filling me,
though there are times of doubt
as hollow as the Grand Canyon,
still God is filling me.
—Anne Sexton

1

My Very Own Financial Crisis

The Child we seek
doesn't need our gold
On love, on love alone
he will build his kingdom.
His pierced hand will hold no scepter,
his haloed head will wear no crown;
his might will not be built
on your toil.
Swifter than lightning
he will soon walk among us.
He will bring us new life
and receive our death,
and the keys to his city
belong to the poor.

—"Love Alone" from *Amahl and the Night Visitors*,
by Gian Carlo Menotti

When I was young, we lived next door to my grandfather, Clair, an Iowa farmer who had a face as leathery as an old boot.

He lived in a 1940s brick bungalow that smelled of cigarette smoke and fried eggs. My grandmother had died of cancer three months before I was born, so my grandfather lived alone. It was a ritual: every evening after dinner, my mother would fix a plate for my grandfather—piled with leftover mashed potatoes, roast, green beans from our garden—and wrap it with foil. Then she would ask one of us kids to run across the yard to my grandpa's house to deliver it. If I made the delivery, I ran in the grass in my bare feet. I'd find

1

Grandpa sitting in his living room in his faux-leather recliner, smoking a cigarette and watching TV. He'd smile. I'd give him a hug, feeling his bony arms and hunched back and his thick, wiry white hair against my cheek. We'd sit in silence as he ate his mashed potatoes, and we watched the news together.

I remember my tenth birthday. I am a tomboy, with skinned knees, and calluses on my feet from going barefoot all spring. My birthday is in May, and my mother has baked an angel food cake with chocolate frosting. We gather in the dining room. My parents and siblings sing the Happy Birthday song. My grandfather slumps in a chair in the corner, his bony legs crossed, observing the celebration. As with every other birthday, he has something for me: a crisp one-hundred-dollar bill. I don't know where he gets his money. He doesn't live like a rich man. He drives a junk heap of a car and never buys new clothes. But every Christmas and birthday, he gives each of his grandkids this treasure, a one-hundred dollar bill. He never says much. But this is his way of telling me he loves me.

After the party, my stomach stuffed with spaghetti and cake, I take my possessions to my room, the room with the yellow shag carpet and gingham curtains. I sleep on the bottom bunk. I pull out a shoe box from underneath the bed, where I keep all of my treasures. Then I take the envelope with the hundred-dollar bill and put it in the box. I feel rich.

Now, thirty-five years later, I long to feel rich again.

Since I've been an adult, somewhere along the way I became obsessed with money. More specifically, I've become obsessed with not having enough.

Lately I've realized that my relationship with money has been an intricate dance of love, hate, envy, fear, anxiety, security, freedom, desire, and repulsion.

All I want is to have peace.

I wore red cowboy boots the day I was laid off, in early 2009. Chicago, like most other cities and towns around the country, was purging itself after a huge feast. In the twenty years I had lived there, it had been on a building binge, with new condo high-rises, shiny skyscrapers, and office buildings popping up on every block. Friends bought homes and sold them for twice as much a few years later. Jobs were easy to come by, and consumption was unapologetic, the ritzy stores along Michigan Avenue—also called The Magnificent Mile—gorged with shoppers and tourists.

Now the binge was over. Half-built condos sat empty, and developers were now resorting to bribing prospective buyers with flat-screen TVs. Housing prices deflated like a wilting helium balloon, and stores were suddenly empty, the sales clerks wandering around the overstuffed racks, bored and purposeless. Chicago purged its offices of workers like me—a midlevel copywriter at a creative agency that suddenly had 50 percent less work than the year before—and we streamed out of loft office buildings, corporate cubicles, and glassy corner offices, dazed, confused, and scared.

Before Christmas, the owner of the small agency had held a quarterly all-company meeting. He had told us that the company was doing well, had no debt, and was, in fact, looking to possibly acquire a smaller agency. Things were looking good.

But a few weeks later, in January, our largest client, a Fortune 500 company, was panicking. The financial industry was in dire straits. Decisions made by powerful CEOs in corner offices were now trickling down to me.

I was glad I wore the red boots. I had always felt a little more confident in them. Powerful. More myself. And I looked at the red tips of the boots as my boss gave me the bad news. I couldn't bear to look at him. His voice trembled. I was the person who wrote copy for the financial clients, the industry that was the worst hit by the recession.

I had been working there for only a year. I was highly paid. It made sense that I would be the one to go.

My boss tried to come off as caring. Maybe he was. He said he would help me any way he could. He would give me a reference. I started feeling sorry for him. Sweat formed on his forehead.

Then he bluntly told me to leave my keys on my desk.

It took my breath away.

I had been clinging to that job the way a baby clings to his mother on the first day of preschool. Now I was being ripped from the safe, comfortable arms of employment.

The timing was bad. My husband, David, was finishing up a master's degree and was working only part-time. We were in the process of adopting a child from Ethiopia. We had plans—plans that disintegrated as soon as my boss told me to leave my keys on my desk.

I didn't say anything as I rose from the couch and walked out the door of my boss's office. I slinked back to my desk, wondering if my colleagues knew what had just happened. They did. I was only one of several who were laid off, so the word had spread around our small office, muffled sobs coming from various areas around the loft space. In the months following, the company would go through two more rounds of layoffs.

I quickly trashed personal files from my computer as I swallowed my panic and tears. I called David on my cell phone and whispered, "I just got laid off!!"

"What?! I can't hear you!" he yelled back into the phone. *"I just got laid off!"* I whispered, more loudly.

"Oh boy," David said. "It's okay, honey. Just come home."

I couldn't hold back the tears any longer. My eyes blurred as I tried to clear my hard drive. I opened my desk drawers and stuffed personal belongings—extra shoes, a cardigan, old *New Yorker* magazines I read on my commute, and framed photos of my family—into my backpack. There wasn't enough room. My fellow writer, Erica, came over and offered to help. "I'm so sorry!" she said.

My now former employer was looking out from his glassed office at those of us who were laid off, as we were trying to make an escape for the door and to the unknown.

Then I packed my possessions in my backpack, hugged the fellow writers who sat in my area and who by that time had discovered my misfortune, and left the building.

On the train ride home I let my tears flow freely. The commuters on the five-o'clock el regarded me strangely, looking like swaddled babies, their faces poking out of their North Face down comforter-like parkas. But I didn't care. "I WAS JUST LAID OFF, AND ALL MY DREAMS ARE DYING!" I wanted to shout.

Instead, I just whimpered in the cold plastic train seat as I watched the lights of the buildings outside go by. I clutched my backpack, the one David had gotten me for Christmas to more easily carry my belongings on my commute each day. Now I wondered if I could return the hundred-dollar bag. It would buy a week's worth of groceries.

I received only two weeks' severance pay. My husband was in school, almost finished with his degree, but his schedule didn't allow him much time to work.

I was scared.

The first few weeks of my unemployment were a blur. Anyone who finds herself unemployed in a recession knows what this is like. And this wasn't just any recession. Companies, at least in my industry, were Totally. Freaked. Out. They were shedding jobs as fast as my cat sheds fur.

I've always prided myself on being able to figure out a way to make money. I've been supporting myself since I was twenty-five. I've suffered through mind-numbing temp jobs, worked as an office manager, and worked for an insurance company. I've freelanced and written copy for real estate firms, ad agencies, publishing houses, websites, and financial companies.

But this time it felt different. I heard that even Starbucks was being inundated with job applications. If I couldn't even land a job at Starbucks because of the glut of out-of-work Chicagoans, then things were pretty bad.

I became obsessed with math and time. How much longer until we ran out of money in our savings account? How much longer could we pay the mortgage? How many days until I got my measly unemployment check in the mail? The checks helped, of course, but barely covered our grocery expenses. And sitting for hours in an unemployment office dealing with belligerent bureaucrats is enough to make anyone start pounding the pavement.

I tried to do some freelance work, what little was out there. But if I made too much, the unemployment checks would stop coming, and then on the weeks I didn't make any money freelancing, I'd have to go back to the unemployment office and start the whole process again. This meant hours sitting in the molded plastic chairs, waiting for my name to be called.

I tried to create a routine: Wake up. Drink coffee. Send my husband off to school. Search online for jobs. Send out resumes. Contact anyone I knew who might help me network. Go for a walk. Then try not to freak out.

But still. There were weeks when we ran low on food, digging through the back of the cupboards to see if there was a stray can of beans or soup.

I took out cash advances on my credit card to pay the mortgage.

I took money out of my (small) 401(k) to pay our taxes in April.

David and I started picturing living in the basement of my father's townhouse.

We debated whether or not to ask for more money from family members.

Things were bad. Financial guru Suze Orman would have been mortified. Dave Ramsey, too. But more than that—*I* was mortified.

How did I get here, at this point in my life, in such a fragile financial state, wondering where the next paycheck would come from?

David tried to comfort me. If he was freaked out, he didn't let me know. Instead, he was totally Zen. "We'll be all right. Let's just take it one day at time," he said as we sat entwined on the couch, discussing our predicament.

But at the time, I was having none of it. I was looking ten years into the future, and my whole world was crashing down around me. "I don't want to take it ONE DAY AT A TIME!" I yelled. I pulled myself off the couch and stomped away.

As David was taking it one day at a time, I was trying to figure out ways to scrape together enough money to pay the mortgage. We humbly accepted help from family, and I started looking around at our possessions, wondering what we could sell to come up with grocery money. How much could I get for that collection of Jadeite glassware? The antique church pew my parents had given me? My wedding ring? When you start thinking of selling family heirlooms, you know things are bad.

But, oddly, in brief moments when I wasn't panicked, I felt a strange sense of calm.

I had always been obsessed with money—specifically, of not having enough. And here I was, unemployed, in debt, weary, and afraid. Basically, what I had always feared would happen, had happened. Short of living on the streets, we were pretty close to having no safety net underneath us.

I knew that something was going to have to change, if we survived this.

├─────────────┤

In my Baptist upbringing, memorizing verses was a weekly ritual in the Sunday school class of our small country church. One I remember learning was John 10:10, "I came that they may have life, and have it abundantly."

My life didn't feel very abundant at the moment.

I had been working so hard for years to create abundance for myself. I worked hard to pay off debt, to have financial security, to have a nice home, a reliable car, and clothes that made me feel good about myself.

But to be honest, my hard work hadn't gotten me very far. I had nagging credit-card debt that I could never seem to shake. I married a wonderful man who was creative, deep, and emotionally and spiritually present but had brought some tax debt into our marriage. We had been faithfully trying to pay it off since we got married.

It's not as if we hadn't tried. I attended a financial workshop at my church. I read books by Suze Orman and Dave Ramsey. I tried, as Dave Ramsey says, to "run like a gazelle" and be free from debt. I cut back on purchasing clothes and lattes. David tried, too. We watched movies on a hand-me-down TV that wasn't hooked up to cable, the color contrast so bad we couldn't make out the subtitles on the DVDs we rented from the artsy video store (instead of going to the movie theater, to save money).

And yet, every time we felt that we were conquering our debt and finding some stability, something happened. Our Jetta broke down what seemed like every other month (those German car parts are dang expensive). Our ten-year-old car was bankrupting us. We had medical bills. Even with insurance, copayments and deductibles added up. I suffered from migraines, and my medication alone cost more than a hundred dollars a month.

We made choices, too. David went back to school to find a more stable career after years of working as a freelance journalist for various newspapers—an industry that was in dire straits.

Now I was exhausted. Tired of trying, of slogging away on the treadmill trying to stay ahead, of trying to create abundance all on my own. It wasn't working.

Something was telling me that, in my quest to find abundance, I had totally missed the point.

⊢────────────┤

David and I went to a church retreat. We had been attending Mass at Old St. Patrick's Church, a Catholic congregation in downtown Chicago, for a few years. Every time the retreat was announced at Mass, we would look at each other and say, "We should go to that." But the timing never seemed right. The retreats were held three times a year, and now that we were going through this crisis, we thought it might be a good time to go, despite the fact that we had limited funds to pay for it. We were weary, and we wanted to get to know other people at the church, to build a community there.

We drove to the retreat center on a Friday night, tired and a little nervous. We followed the signs for the retreat through the winding roads. We had no idea what to expect, and we were skeptical.

"What are we going to do, sit around a fire and sing 'Kumbaya'?" David asked.

I was imagining awkward times of "sharing." I was mostly hoping I could just walk in the woods, take naps, and meet some nice people. I was weary and wanted rest.

We arrived late. We opened the car doors, and immediately someone was there to help us carry our bags.

"No, I got it. Really," I said, heaving my bulky suitcase out of the trunk. But the retreat staff-person, some stranger with a quirky smile and black curly hair, gently pushed me aside and took my bag from me.

Another person—a woman half my size—carried David's bag. We walked self-consciously alongside them into the dorm building where we were bunking for the weekend.

After dropping off our bags, our hosts led us into a conference room that was lit with candles. There were about fifty people in the room. We sat at a table with six other people.

Terry, the director of adult spiritual formation at the church, was in charge. He was in his fifties, had a kind face, and described himself as "the short, white, chubby guy." He wore a crucifix around his neck and Birkenstock sandals on his feet. With white socks.

Like the first time David and I had walked into Old Saint Pat's a few years before and felt that we had come home, the minute I stepped into the candlelit room, I knew this was where I belonged that weekend. I sank down in the folding chair, and my body seemed to let go of all the stress I had been feeling for months.

As candles burned on the tables and the moonlight shone through the windows, forming blue rectangles on the carpet, we heard stories. Stories of people who had been through difficult times but were able to somehow see God in the midst of them.

One story in particular stayed with me. Bob and Jill told of falling in love, of having two daughters, and then, about how one of their daughters, as a freshman in college, had been sexually assaulted. Later, depressed and unable to shake the horrible experience, she accidentally overdosed on medication and died.

As I listened to their story, I also noticed the joy and peace I saw on their faces. How could they be so joyful despite their suffering? This was something I wanted.

In the months after their daughter's death, Jill and Bob took ballroom dancing lessons. It was something they'd always wanted to do. The timing seemed a little crazy, but they knew that they had to get out of the house and participate in life somehow, even though they didn't really want to. Their daughter had been a dancer, and they thought this would be a good way to honor her life. So they forced themselves to go to classes every week. But soon, they found themselves practicing their steps in their garage. They explained that it was the only time that they found themselves—if only a tiny bit—lifted out of their bone-crushing grief.

At the end of their talk, Bob walked over to a CD player and turned on some music, and there, in the middle of the conference room filled with tables of retreat participants, they danced. I looked at the joy and peace on their faces and saw that they had somehow, inexplicably, found abundance in the ugliness and pain of life. Now they were dancing. I was crying.

I couldn't imagine how they could experience such pain and still find joy. I had caught glimpses of that joy. But every time I felt I had found this abundance, it had wriggled free from my grasp, like the wet sunfish I used to catch with a cane pole when fishing with Grandpa. I would catch one and free it from the metal hook, feeling the gristle of the fish's lips, and then it would flop in my hands and plop back into the pond.

That's what life seemed to be doing to me. I couldn't imagine hanging on to abundance long enough to feel real peace. Or to dance in the middle of a room filled with strangers.

But I wanted to know what Bob and Jill knew.

Why do people suffer? Why were we going through this financial crisis? Was there meaning in it? And would we come out the other side, as had these people who were telling their stories? Richard Rohr says,

We are at a symbolic disadvantage as a wealthy culture. Jesus said that the rich man or woman will find it hard to understand what he is talking about. The rich can satisfy their loneliness and longing in false ways, in quick fixes that avoid the necessary learning. In terms of soul work, we dare not get rid of the pain before we have learned what it has to teach us. That's why the poor have a head start. . . . They remain empty whether they want to or not. . . . We must go inside the belly of the whale for a while. Then and only then will we be spit upon a new shore and understand our call.[1]

The next morning at the retreat, I woke up early and walked down to the lake to watch the sun rise. It was so quiet. The sun was coming up, but I was freezing. The lake was frozen, and Canada geese were honking quietly or roosting on the ice with their beaks tucked into their wings to keep warm. I saw a six-point buck lazily wandering off into the trees. I waited for the sun.

The sun's coming seemed to take forever, and I almost gave up and walked back to our dorm room to get warm. But the colors in the sky kept changing, and I was mesmerized. The colors of the sky just before sunrise or sunset are more beautiful than the colors of the actual event. As I waited for the sun and watched the sky changing, I prayed that something good would come out of the darkness.

2

Looking for Blessings in All the Wrong Places

The little country Baptist church my family attended until I was twelve had wooden pews and sculpted green carpet that formed a path up the aisle, and smelled of Pledge, grape juice, and air freshener. In the summer, I wore flowered sundresses to church—dresses sewn by my mother—with rickrack around the hem and lace on the shoulder straps. The church wasn't air-conditioned, and during the humid, Midwestern summers my bare legs would stick to the gooey varnish on the pews.

My ancestors founded that church in the mid-1800s. Generations of my family had worshipped there, first when it was a Congregational church, and later, maybe around 1968 or so, when it turned into a Baptist church.

We could see the Adelphi Calvary Baptist Church from our house. We lived in an old, beautiful farmhouse that was built in 1917. It had a broad front porch that was held up by four pillars and looked out across the Des Moines River valley. It was exactly one mile east of the church. My grandfather was born in the house, in the bedroom where my sister and I shared bunk beds. Halfway between the church and our old farmhouse was an eighty-acre plot of land where my ancestors first settled when they came over from Scotland in 1864.

From my bedroom window I could see the church steeple reaching into the clear blue, Iowa summer sky. The steeple was like a compass, pointing us in the right direction.

The church was the foundation for the rhythm of our lives. For Sunday morning Sunday school, Sunday service, Sunday evening service and youth group, and Wednesday night prayer meetings, we would pile into the car and make the short trek up the hill to church. Mom played the piano and organ during church services, her beehive hairdo bobbing up and down as she pushed the foot pedals, and Dad, with his skinny ties and dark suits, was a deacon. In Sunday school, my Aunt Colleen told us Bible stories, placing flannel characters on the cheesy flannel background as she told about Daniel and the lions' den, Joseph and the coat of many colors, and the prodigal son who decided to return home after resorting to eating slop from the pigs' trough.

Wednesday night prayer meetings or Sunday evening services typically involved sing-alongs. Before gathering in small groups to pray for the ill, infirm, or prodigal members of the congregation, and before testimony time, when congregants stood up, as the spirit led, to tell their stories of God in their lives, we would have a time of old-fashioned hymn singing. The pastor, who was also the de facto worship leader, wore a cheap, brown polyester suit with a thick tie, his hands gripping the sides of the pulpit. "Just call out a page number from the hymnal!" he would belt out.

"Hymn number 325!" my uncle Jim would yell from the back of the church. "OK, then," said Pastor John. "All together now, let's sing 'Blessed Assurance'!" My mom played a four-measure introduction, and we all started singing, a little shakily at first, but then more fully when we got to the chorus, and with conviction we raised our voices to the heavens.

I remember singing all the old hymns during these hymn sings. One of my favorites went like this:

Count your blessings, name them one by one
Count your blessings, see what God hath done.
Count your blessings, name them one by one.
Count your many blessings, see what God hath done!

As I sang melody, then harmony, blending my voice with the voices of those people I loved and who were a part of our small community, I felt warm and secure, knowing that I had this loving community around me, and a loving God who would bestow blessings on me throughout my life.

We knew the answers. We were confident in our faith. Everything was black and white.

Until one day, many years later, when things weren't black and white anymore.

Inevitably, reality crashed into my simplistic beliefs. The cracks started showing in college. "What if we're all on this train, and we're telling everyone else to get on board, and we're so convinced that this is the best train and we're going to this really great place, but in reality, it's going nowhere?" my college friend, Jon, a missionary kid, asked me one day, as we sat on a park bench on the Baptist college campus. His words fueled my doubts and left me shaken.

In philosophy class, we talked about epistemology, and how we know what we know, and our class discussions made me wonder, *How do we know the Scripture is true? How do we know God exists?*

The first time I asked a question like this was when I was six or so and I asked my mother, "Mom, how do we know the Bible is true?" I yelled this at her from the dining room, where I was playing with my dolls. She was fixing green beans and meatloaf in the kitchen. Apparently, dressing Ken and Barbie and putting them in the Barbie

Malibu Dream House had inspired me to contemplate the existence of God and the truth of the Bible. Mom poked her head around the corner, a wooden spoon in her hand.

She looked at me and said, kindly yet definitively, "Well, it just is." And then went back to cooking dinner.

Most of my questions in the little Baptist church, and later, in a bigger Baptist church, were met with similar responses. The underlying message was that questioning was not allowed. So I didn't ask many questions again, although they remained in my soul. My questions scared people.

But now, as life went on, these questions were becoming more and more heavy.

The easy faith of "Count Your Blessings" rang through my head until one day, I didn't feel so blessed. I felt I had no "blessings" to count.

Getting laid off from my job was the last straw. I talked to my sister on the phone, and she said "Why do these things always happen to you?!"

"I don't know," I sighed. And I really didn't.

I could relate to the Arthur character in the Coen brothers' movie *A Serious Man*. Arthur is the main character's brother and is down on his luck. He has a boil on his neck that he spends hours in the bathroom trying to drain. He's not married, is unemployed, and apparently is homeless, because he's sleeping on his brother, Larry's, sofa. He's socially awkward and in trouble with the law.

He complains to his brother about *HaShem* (a word Jews use for God). "HaShem hasn't given me shit!" he sobs to his brother one night, when he's at his wits' end. Larry tries to comfort him by saying, "You know, sometimes we have to help ourselves," but his comfort and advice seem empty because Larry feels abandoned by God, too. All they can do in the end is embrace one another and cry.

In the days after my layoff, I felt just like Arthur. I felt that God had given me nothing.

Life seemed unfair and random. My doubts started resurfacing.

Unfortunately, the chorus of that old hymn didn't specify how to get the blessings we all want. *Count your blessings, name them one by one.* It sounds as if collecting blessings is as easy as getting candy on Halloween—don a costume, knock on a few doors, and at the end of the night, you go home and count your miniboxes of Milk Duds and Snickers bars.

I started thinking about these blessings that I felt God hadn't given to me. I didn't want to end up like Arthur, feeling forsaken and that "God hadn't given me shit."

I had a litany of questions that had been building up my whole life and were now coming to the surface:

- How could a God who loves justice seem to have such an unjust way of giving those he loves "blessings?"

- Why does he bless some couples with children, while others wait as each month goes by without a positive pregnancy test?

- Why does God give some people financial security, while others, who work just as hard and seem just as deserving, are caught in a perfect storm of job layoffs, unexpected medical expenses, and car repairs?

- Why does God allow a friend who's just shy of forty to die of breast cancer, while the rest of us remain healthy?

- Why does God give some people steady work, while others spend months or years in unemployment?

People in my Christian community seemed to throw around the word *blessing* with impunity, as if it were a gold star sticker for jumping through all the right hoops.

Shortly after I was laid off, I attended my women's group—a gathering of women I knew from my former church and other places. One member of the group mentioned how she felt guilty that her family was flush with cash while someone like me was struggling just to pay the mortgage.

This friend and her husband had done all the right things with their finances: they had paid off their mortgage, saved a bundle, stuck to a budget, and gone without. They had managed their money well and were reaping the benefits.

But someone in the group made a comment that made me cringe. "God has blessed you," she said to our financially well-off member.

I almost choked on my latte. "Really?" I blurted. "Is that a 'blessing' from God?" And as the discussion went on, I had other questions, such as, "What about other people who have done everything right and have gotten laid off or had medical expenses that they can't pay or don't have family who can help them out from time to time? Are God's blessings a result of our doing everything right? And what about the people in third-world countries who work day and night just to survive? Why do they not seem to get a blessing from God?"

The late Mike Yaconelli, former editor of *The Wittenberg Door*, a Christian satirical magazine, once wrote:

> I've heard God credited for getting new cars, new houses, new clothes, even new girlfriends. What I would like to know is why God is so good at providing new cars and boats and so bad at feeding most of the world. I think the answer is obvious. God isn't the infinite Santa Claus. God doesn't give people material abundance as a reward for serving him. We have taken our material-obsessed mentality and tried to make the Christian faith compatible with it. That just doesn't work. Material abundance says nothing about God's blessing, and we dare not equate the two.

In the movie *A Serious Man*, the main character, Larry Gopnik, finds himself in a Job-like situation. His life is crumbling around him. His wife is divorcing him, his teaching career is threatened by a disgruntled student who is trying to blackmail him into giving him a better grade, and his children are spoiled and whiny. But he's been a *serious man*. He's done everything right. So why are these things happening to him?

He asks his rabbis, who sit behind big, oak desks. One has a white beard that stretches like cotton candy down to his chest. Each of them pontificates while Larry looks at them, befuddled. Rabbis are supposed to have answers, and he's incredulous that they have no answers.

Like Larry, I felt that *HaShem* wasn't holding up his end of the bargain, and no one seemed to be able to answer my questions.

A few years ago, I ran into my former youth pastor. I hadn't seen him in several years. Mike's an adventurer. With his wiry, athletic frame and curly blond hair, he could appear on the cover of *Outside* magazine. He's traveled all over the world, helping out in orphanages and photographing situations and people in third-world countries.

Fresh out of college thirty-five years ago, he landed a job as pastor of our youth group. He was funny, smart, and adventurous. Each year, Mike threw a dart at a map, and that's where we would take a missions trip that year. We went to the back hills of Kentucky to help out poor, struggling churches, and to an Indian reservation in the mountains of Montana.

He loved his family; he and his wife had three daughters, and, in his words, he "did everything right" by being a youth pastor, providing for his family, and being a godly man.

But then he found out that his wife was leaving him.

As I had lunch with him one day, we talked about how he was going through a crisis of faith. "I thought I was doing everything right," he said. "And look what happened. Sometimes I don't know what I believe about God anymore. It just doesn't make sense."

One Webster's dictionary defines a blessing as "a declaration of divine favor, or an invocation imploring divine favor on someone or something." It's also a "means of happiness; that which promotes prosperity and welfare; a beneficent gift."

"Very important," says theologian Fred Craddock, "is the recognition that the beatitudes appear at the beginning of the Sermon on the Mount, before a single instruction is given, before there has been time for obedience or disobedience. If the blessings were only for the deserving, very likely they would be stated at the end of the sermon, probably prefaced with the conditional clause, 'If you have done all these things.' *But appearing at the beginning, they say that God's favor precedes all our endeavors.*"

The other day, I heard one of my favorite priests, Father Cusick, remind us that the Beatitudes tell us that we are *already* blessed. We don't have to do anything to earn it. Those who mourn. Those who wait. Those who are in debt. Those who struggle. Those who are poor. Those people—we—are already blessed.

"What would this world be like if each of us woke up in the morning, looked in the mirror, and told the reflection, 'You are blessed!'?" asked Fr. Cusick. "Would we walk around differently, knowing that we already have God's blessing? Would we start seeing things differently?"

I could do as my priest suggested, and wake up every morning and tell myself in the mirror that God loves me—but would it really work?

So I started thinking that maybe I was thinking about blessings all wrong.

One day, I sat in my therapist's office complaining about my state of affairs. I was unemployed. We were thousands of dollars in debt, and my job prospects were bleak, with the economy tanking. And besides all that, our adoption was starting to look like a pipe dream. With our precarious financial situation, my unemployment, the fact that David was still in school, and our increasing ages, we weren't the best candidates to become adoptive parents.

"I've got nothing," I said to Chris, my therapist. "What's up with that? Why can't God give me a break?" I felt that my back was against the wall and I was stuck in a hopeless situation, with all my dreams dying.

In his typical fashion, Chris thought for a moment. Then he said, "Well, all of these blessings you think other people are getting—you know, sometimes they end up not to be blessings at all."

As I thought about his comment, I realized he was right.

My friends, Jane and Andy, struggled with infertility for years. Finally, they had the opportunity to adopt an adorable baby boy, right around the time she found out she was pregnant. It seemed that God was blessing them! *Hurray! God is good after all!* we all thought.

But a few months after the birth of their baby girl, they found out that she has a major heart defect and a genetic disorder called 22q11.2 deletion syndrome. The little girl has had several open-heart surgeries. But her arteries are so small (because of the defect) that the doctors are not sure if they will ever be able to totally "fix" her heart. So Jane and Andy are living constantly with the fear that their daughter may not make it through the next heart surgery or that she'll outgrow her heart before a solution is found.

What happened to the blessing?

As I thought about my therapist's words, I realized I had seen this scenario play out many times.

Friends who had been "blessed" with a child later had their hearts broken by that child, or parenthood had left them emotionally and spiritually depleted. Other friends who had been financially success-ful realized that money didn't satisfy their deepest longings after all. Long-awaited marriages had sometimes ended in divorce.

So if what we think is a blessing sometimes turn out to not be a blessing at all, then maybe the opposite was true.

When I read the Beatitudes again, I realized that they're not what you'd expect. The groups of people I often think of as "blessed" in our contemporary society—the wealthy, the happy, the assertive, and the powerful—are not those whom Jesus was naming as blessed. Instead, he said:

> Blessed are the poor in spirit, for theirs is the kingdom of heaven.
> Blessed are those who mourn, for they shall be comforted.
> Blessed are the gentle, for they shall inherit the earth.
> Blessed are those who hunger and thirst for righteousness, for they
> shall be satisfied.
> Blessed are the merciful, for they shall receive mercy.
> Blessed are the pure in heart, for they shall see God.
> Blessed are the peacemakers, for they shall be called sons of God.
> Blessed are those who have been persecuted for the sake of
> righteousness, for theirs is the kingdom of heaven.
> Blessed are you when people insult you and persecute you, and
> falsely say all kinds of evil against you because of Me.
> Rejoice and be glad, for your reward in heaven is great; for in the
> same way they persecuted the prophets who were before you.
>
> —New American Standard Bible

Slowly, I was learning to look at blessings differently, in the intan-gible things: the growth I saw in someone who had struggled; the compassion that was growing in me for those who had even less in their bank account than I did; the great love and perseverance of par-ents who were raising a sick child.

Author Rob Bell, during a book tour in Chicago, said, "You can have great wealth and possess nothing. You can own nothing yet possess the universe. . . . Sometimes you lose something, but you find something more valuable." Then, "Pain is a gift. Sometimes it takes something painful to wake us up to how much we have to possess."

We see through a glass darkly. It's all murky, the hows and whys. Someday we will understand. In the midst of this desert, I look for God in the small things. Faith means believing, even when you can't see. I look at my flowers on my small deck of our condo and see the little sprouts of yellow on my snapdragons, and the deep purples of my pansies as they turn their petals to the morning sun. *Is that you God? Are you even there?* I whisper into the air.

We try to make sense of it all, but in this chaos, I want to be okay with it not making sense. Of living in the chaos and uncertainty and insecurity, and still trusting God that we'll be okay. Of seeing what seems unfair, and realizing that maybe there's something more going on that I can't understand.

I heard novelist Mary Doria Russell interviewed by Krista Tippett on National Public Radio's *Speaking of Faith*. She said, "God paints on a vast canvas, and his paintbrush is time." Often, we don't know if something is a blessing or not until much later.

I recently googled the old hymn I remembered singing at Adelphi Calvary Baptist Church so long ago, and I realized that maybe the theology wasn't as far off as I thought. The hymn acknowledges that God's blessings come in the turmoil of life, just when we're thinking that God doesn't love us.

Yes, this is where I find myself now. And as corny as the words are, I hear the verses in my head:

When upon life's billows you are tempest-tossed,
When you are discouraged, thinking all is lost,

Count your many blessings, name them one by one,
And it will surprise you what the Lord hath done
So, amid the conflict whether great or small,
Do not be discouraged, God is over all;
Count your many blessings, angels will attend
Help and comfort give you to your journey's end.

These days, I'm thinking that when all is said and done, I may look back and see the blessings clearly and will be surprised at what the Lord has done.

HaShem, give me help and comfort to the journey's end.

3
Hail Mary, Full of Grace

Hold fast to dreams
For if dreams die
Life is a broken-winged bird
That cannot fly.

—Langston Hughes

About six months after my layoff, as I was still looking for work, and our adoption was still on hold, and I was still scrambling to pay the mortgage and other bills, I took a walk with my friend Kate. We were at the University of Saint Mary of the Lake, where David and I had attended the retreat shortly after my layoff. This time, I was there to staff the retreat, and it was a beautiful spring day, although still a little chilly.

The sprawling campus is filled with lovely old, neo-Classical buildings, beautiful statues, icons of saints, Jesus, and Mary, and surrounded by woods filled with roaming deer, beaver, and other wildlife. I felt as if I were at a monastery.

Kate's new baby was in a stroller.

At one point in our walk, we stopped by a grotto that held a statue of Mary.

"Wait, I want to stop here for a minute," Kate said. She pulled a note out of her pocket and stuck it between two stones in the grotto. She silently prayed for a moment; then we resumed our walk. I pulled my jacket tighter around me.

"What was that all about?" I asked.

Kate knows I'm not a cradle Catholic. I grew up Baptist. And Baptists don't "believe" in Mary. She's just a character in the Christmas story who appears around Christmastime and then goes away the rest of the year.

And I certainly didn't have any experience with grottos of the Madonna. My Baptist mother would be turning over in her grave.

"You know, before I got pregnant, I prayed to Mary, and I think maybe she had something to do with me getting pregnant. So I just wanted to thank her," Kate said.

All of this talk about Mary made me uncomfortable.

Mary is the one part of the Catholic tradition that I've kept at arm's length since David and I started going to Old St. Pat's. I don't believe she can really hear my prayers, and I'm a little confused about why Catholics make such a big deal out of her. But I was too embarrassed to admit this to Kate, so I just played along and said, "Oh, how nice."

Can Mary help us petition God to answer our prayers? Is she our advocate? Is she somehow divine? And more than anything, can she help bring a child into my life and fulfill my dream of becoming a mother?

I don't know what to think of this information from Kate. And yet, Kate got pregnant at age forty-five. She gave birth to a perfectly healthy baby girl and named her Faith. I had been humbled in the past six months. Who was I to say Mary didn't have something to do with Kate's having a child?

Since marrying in 2005, David and I had been trying to add a child to our family as well. But our financial difficulties had pushed that desire into limbo.

The recession and my unemployment were more than just a temporary setback that could be fixed with a bit of frugality and a few weeks of strategically sending résumés to possible employers—résumés that blew silently like tumbleweeds across the windswept emptiness of the job market.

There was something much deeper rumbling in my soul: a realization that my heart was withering and that my dream of becoming a mother was dying a long, slow death.

I've never been one of those women for whom becoming a mom was an all-consuming goal and passion. In my twenties and early thirties, I had enjoyed the single life, flying to Mexico with girlfriends for weeklong vacations, stumbling through career and dating relationships, and basically "finding myself." I yearned to be married, sure, but there were also times when I liked the freedom of being single. My three older sisters had young children. I knew it was hard work.

But by the time I was thirty-five and still single, I starting thinking about the possibility of becoming a mother. While I loved my freedom, I also had always pictured myself with a child. The single life and my career were becoming less fulfilling to me. I wanted some solid ground, some stability, some people around me—in close proximity—to love.

I worked hard to fill my life with other things. I sponsored a refugee family with four little girls. I volunteered at an animal shelter. I flew to Kosovo and Mexico on mission trips to work in orphanages. All of these things helped to ease the emptiness I felt in my life.

But I wanted a husband and a child of my own to love and protect and nurture.

I always thought I would have that opportunity. Even as the years ticked by, I pictured myself with a little girl. I have ten nephews and three nieces. We needed more girls in the family. So I thought it would be nice to provide my family with another girl, whether through birth or adoption (two of my beautiful nieces are adopted from China).

When I was thirty-eight, my gynecologist explained to me that "thirty-eight-year-old eggs are better than forty-year-old eggs," so would I want to freeze my eggs just in case I wanted to get pregnant a few years from now? "No," I told her confidently. "I don't want to freeze my eggs, because if I can't have biological children, I would be very happy adopting."

Two years later, my forty-year-old eggs and I got married.

We were optimistic.

I knew plenty of friends who had had children after age forty with no problem. Or at least with a little bit of help from the fertility specialist. Back then, I wasn't yet a Catholic, so neither David nor I thought twice about getting technological help to conceive. It seemed perfectly doable.

Sure enough, the July after we got married, I took a home pregnancy test and saw the little blue line on the stick appear, as if saying, *Yes, all your waiting was worth it. Your marriage has been "blessed."*

It also seemed like a ticket to no longer feeling like an anomaly, to having something to talk about with my other childbearing friends, to not feeling like the odd person out at family gatherings and not feeling sad at a Mother's Day church service.

I think David and I were a little surprised and afraid, too. I was afraid of losing the body I'd been trying to diet and torture into shape at the gym for years. I watched in horror as my abdomen thickened and my size-8 Gap Long and Lean jeans didn't fit anymore.

And I think we were both afraid of what parenthood would entail. We were afraid of the unknown. We didn't feel settled in our careers. David had long been thinking about going back to school to train as a psychotherapist.

Plus, we hadn't even known each other for a year yet. It was all moving too fast. We were, needless to say, a little bit freaked out. But also giddily excited.

I wore a black poncho to work and felt as if I were hiding a very precious secret—this beautiful creature, my child, growing inside of me.

David and I would go through our days thinking of names. He would e-mail me at work. "How about Judith? It's a family name."

"No," I would write back. "I like Judith, but I'm sure everyone would call her 'Judy,' and I don't like Judy!"

I started a list of names in my journal:

- Sean

- Robert

- Alexandra

- Fiona

- Maura

- Lauren

"All the numbers look good," said my ob-gyn. "The pregnancy is strong."

At six weeks, I went to get an ultrasound. I heard the heartbeat: *twirp, twirp, twirp, twirp.* Like a tiny bird. There it was on the computer screen. The technician printed out a picture of my baby. It looked like a blob to me, but after showing it to David at home (we were naïve about all the pregnancy protocol and hadn't thought it was important for him to be there when I had the ultrasound), I placed it carefully between the pages of my journal.

The due date was June 28, my father's birthday. Oh, what a gift to my dad—a surprise grandchild, probably his last, after the pain of my mother's death a few years earlier. It was perfect!

I started feeling morning sickness. David and I announced the news to our family and friends. Everyone was happy and surprised.

But at ten weeks, I stopped feeling morning sickness. I was relieved not to be on the verge of vomiting every five minutes, but also a little worried. I felt different.

My friends and sisters kept reassuring me. "Morning sickness usually lasts only the first trimester," my sister said. It made me feel better, thinking that maybe I was less nauseated because I was further along in the pregnancy.

But a week later, my ob-gyn couldn't find the heartbeat on her handheld ultrasound machine. "You know, this machine isn't very strong. I'm sure the baby is just turned at an awkward angle so we can't hear its heartbeat," she said. So she sent me to get a second ultrasound at the hospital, with a bigger, better machine.

But lying on the table in the semidarkness, looking at the young technician's face, there was only silence. No sweet little *twirp, twirp, twirp* coming from my baby's heart.

"I'm sorry," the technician said.

My little bird was gone.

I felt like I couldn't breathe. I looked at the black screen filled with white static and swirls.

She offered to let me use the phone to call the doctor.

I got off the table and wrapped the paper gown around my shoulders. The paper crinkled as I walked. I went into the bathroom to change into my clothes. I looked at myself in the mirror in disbelief. "It's over," I said to my reflection, trying to absorb the news. I felt as if I had been punched in the stomach. I changed my clothes. Then the knot in my stomach pushed itself to the surface. I put my face against the cinder-block wall and sobbed.

I don't know why God "blesses" some with children while others are left feeling the vast, empty hole that barrenness leaves.

I blamed myself. Did I do something to cause the miscarriage? Was it that one time I accidentally took an Ibuprofen because I had a headache? Or did I drink too much caffeine?

Did the baby sense that I was a little freaked out about my jeans getting tighter? I felt guilty for being so selfish. Maybe my little bird didn't feel wanted. Was I too self-centered to be a mother?

I looked at the list of baby names in my journal and realized that we wouldn't need them anymore.

Just a few weeks after we had spread the good news of our pregnancy, we had to tell those same family and friends the sad news that it was over. They sent us sympathetic e-mails and cards.

Slowly, my stomach flattened, and I could fit into my size-8 jeans again. I didn't care.

We tried getting pregnant again after a few months. But the months ticked by, and we weren't getting any younger. I turned forty-two. We were in a race against time.

I was pregnant again that next spring. Briefly. It was barely a pregnancy. I just know I was pregnant and after a few weeks, it was over. My ob-gyn used the term *chemical pregnancy*.

After trying for another six months, we decided to see a fertility specialist.

The doctor took blood tests, and we went through three months of treatment. IVF is not fun. I gave myself shots every day for a month, and then more shots of hormones to boost my egg production. Because of my age, the doctor put me on the highest level of hormones.

Even then, when it came time to retrieve what should have been an abundance of eggs from my ovaries, only one measly egg was retrieved. A few days later, we got the call that the one egg had failed to become an embryo. I knew after that first round of IVF that I didn't want to do it again. It didn't feel right for us.

We had the last meeting with our "reproduction specialist," and she told us in no uncertain terms that I probably wouldn't be able to get pregnant through IVF with my own eggs. Therefore, she suggested donor eggs.

David and I had already discussed this option, and had decided that we'd rather adopt. So in that one meeting, we realized that our quest for a biological child was over.

We walked out of the office, and I looked over at David. He was crying. We waited for the elevator. This wasn't just my dream that was dying—it was his, too. And I felt so powerless to give him a baby.

Because adoption had always been in the backs of our minds, it wasn't hard for us to make the transition.

But still, we mourned. We mourned our little bird. We grieved at the thought of not having a child who looked like us. We felt cheated because we would never have the experience of going through pregnancy and childbirth together.

A friend of mine who got pregnant around the same time that I lost Little Bird gave birth to a little boy, at home, in a birthing pool. She later reported to me that giving birth was a "spiritual experience" for her.

I wondered what amazing experience I was missing out on.

But gradually, our thoughts turned toward adopting a tiny brown-eyed beauty from Ethiopia. We decided to adopt a child who was a little older, maybe age three or four, because those are the children who tend to be passed over because most families want infants. We wanted to provide a home for a child who was less likely to be adopted.

With at least one million AIDS orphans in Ethiopia, we felt that we were not only building a family but also alleviating a small part of the suffering caused by a horrible epidemic.

The only thing standing in our way was money.

While giving birth is expensive, most of the time an insurance policy will pay for giving birth in a hospital. Insurance even paid for our IVF treatments.

For adoption, there's no insurance. We'd have to come up with the $30,000 or more by ourselves to add an Ethiopian child to our family.

At the time, I was still employed. But David was just starting work at Northwestern University toward his master's degree in counseling psychology.

I always thought it would be somewhat easy to adopt. My sisters adopted from China in the 1990s. For them, it was a year from home study to picking up their children. But things have changed. There's a lot more paperwork now, and wait times are getting longer. Much longer.

Even though I worried about adopting a child while David was in school, I was concerned about our getting older. Many countries have age limits. We were reaching the upper limits of the criteria in many countries' adoption policies.

Domestic adoption would be difficult; our adoption counselor told us that most birth mothers would choose younger adoptive parents.

We thought about foster-to-adopt, but that had its own barriers. I didn't know if I could allow myself to get attached to a child, only to have to give that child back to a biological parent who may, or may not, be able to fully parent the child. And most of the children who were truly free for adoption were much older—age eight or nine. Because David and I had never been parents before, we thought this would be difficult.

Ethiopia seemed like the best fit for us. The age limits were flexible, there were many children who needed homes, and it required only one trip and was cheaper than other programs.

Adoption is not cheap. One acquaintance of mine unfairly equated it to "buying a baby." But that's not true at all. In ethical adoptions done through reputable agencies, the money spent goes toward the cost of the adoption: the costs of employing social workers to do our home study, the costs of legal forms, the cost of running the orphanage in the country, and the cost of travel to and from Ethiopia. No one is getting rich from the adoption fees.

One Saturday we stopped at Starbucks for coffee and drove a few miles to the old stone building that housed the adoption agency. The agency was in a suburb near our home. It was reputable, and people told us it was one of the best around.

We were nervous as we approached the old stone castlelike building. We had no idea what to expect. We had already filled out an initial application and completed a form that summarized our finances. We felt that we were good candidates to be adoptive parents. David's sisters had been adopted, as were two of my nieces. So we both had experience being in families where adoption was valued. We thought it beneficial that David was in training to be a therapist; that would better equip us to deal with attachment or grief issues in an adopted child. And even though David was in school, I had a solid job at the time (this was about a year before I got laid off).

We sat across the desk from our adoption counselor. She wasn't the warm, friendly social worker I was expecting. She had black hair and looked warily at us from the reading glasses perched at the end of her sharp nose. She asked us many questions about our families, our background, our jobs, our attitudes about transracial adoption. David and I nervously answered, wondering if our responses were passing muster.

Then she started talking about our "financial picture." "Why did you decide to go back to school?" she asked David. "You were making a good salary. Why do you want to become a therapist and work for less money?"

David nervously tried to answer her question. He was a newspaper journalist and an online editor. He felt that his future job prospects in the journalism field were limited and helping people as a trained therapist would be more fulfilling.

"Well, what about this debt you have? You have $8,000 in credit-card debt. Why don't you have more in savings?"

At this point, my face flushed red with shame. Yes, we had some credit-card debt. Yes, David and I had been somewhat irresponsible with our money in the past, and to be honest, as writers, neither of us had made very much. But we were making progress in getting our finances in order and paying off our debt.

I wasn't expecting this kind of scrutiny.

"I really feel you should get this debt paid off before you adopt," she said. "I don't think this is a good time, especially since David is going back to school. It would be difficult to adopt while he's in school."

With that, she handed us back our $200 check for the registration fee. "It was nice meeting you," she said.

David and I looked at each other and feebly said, "Nice meeting you, too."

We looked at each other as we walked back to our car. "That was brutal," David said.

We didn't say much as we drove home. "Maybe we just aren't meant to be parents," I said. "Maybe we just don't deserve it."

David grabbed my hand.

I felt shame that we didn't make more money. Shame that we had debt. Shame that this stranger had deemed us "unworthy" of adopting a child.

For the first time, I realized that maybe I would never become a mother.

Could I ever feel the fullness of God's love when I felt this huge hole and emptiness inside of me? In my quest to find abundance, I could not reconcile these two things.

Like a child looking in on a party to which she wasn't invited, I watched as friends like Kate gave birth even though they were older, and other friends with more money added children through adoption. Once again, things that seemed so easy for other people seemed so unattainable for me.

In high school, we weren't allowed to go to dances because—well, there would be *dancing*. My strict fundamentalist Baptist upbringing made it seem a certainty that it was a slippery slope from a sock hop to a romp in the bedroom.

When I was a sophomore and my sister was a senior, she was student-body president. One of the responsibilities of her new role was to help plan the Junior-Senior Prom. This presented a problem, as she would not be allowed to attend.

But she did her best to guide the prom committee in the planning stages. The night of the big event, neither of us attended the prom. But she wanted to drive by the school gym to see if the event was running smoothly. So my dad drove me and my sister in his big brown Cadillac to the school that night, and as we crouched down in the backseat so no one could see us, we got a glimpse of the party inside.

The double doors of the gym were open, and there was a warm glow of lights inside. Kids were dancing to the music, having fun, while my sister and I were hunched in the back of my dad's car.

How much of my life had I felt like that awkward, unhappy teen crouched in the back of the Cadillac, unseen as others took part in life's joys and adventures and I just watched.

In my search for abundance, I wrestled with these feelings and thoughts. There had to be an answer, but all I could focus on was that life was not turning out the way I had expected. Abundance, for me, was financial security, but also seeing the fulfillment of a life I had envisioned, dreamed of, and hoped for.

What if that picture never became a reality?

I thought of Mary, and her visit from the angel, telling her that she would bear a son. Pregnant, without being married. So young. In a culture where getting pregnant outside of marriage was a bad, bad thing.

I'm sure it wasn't what she expected. Did she feel as I did—that the story of her life had just taken a tragic turn? That a good ending could not be imagined? That there would always be a sinking feeling of disappointment and disillusionment?

And yet, she trusted. And believed. And moved forward.

Since going to Old St. Pat's, I'd been hearing about Mary from time to time. One of the things I liked most was when Terry Nelson-Johnson talked about how Mary said yes when God asked something big of her.

Can you carry my Son to term and give birth to him in a stable?

"May it be," Mary replied.

In the midst of her fear and trembling and the unknown, she said yes to God.

A few months later, I was visiting Kate at her home when she gave me a brooch with a cameo of the Madonna on it. "Here," she said, "take this." She explained that she had given the brooch to two other friends, both of whom had gotten pregnant. Now she wanted me to have it.

I really doubted that Mary could help me in the baby department. I believed she was the mother of Jesus. But did I believe she could hear my prayers and that she had any pull with Jesus to either (1) perform a miracle and get me pregnant at age forty-five or (2), drop thirty thousand bucks from heaven so we could adopt a child? No.

No, no, no. I didn't believe it. But I took the cameo graciously and gave Kate a hug. At least she was thinking of me.

Then we went back into her living room and played with her beautiful six-month-old daughter. I kissed baby Faith's fingers and touched her toes. I thought about the soft skin of a baby I would never know. Of how old my child would be now.

I do that: I look at four-year-olds at Starbucks and think about what my child would look like now. I'm imagining she's a girl, always a girl. Would she have had my fine hair and green eyes? Or David's dark hair? Would she be shy, like I was when I was four? Would she be bookish and smart? Or artistic and creative?

There would always be an emptiness. I needed to learn how to fill it, or at least how to live with it. Until I could do that, I would never feel that I was living a life of abundance.

And I wondered if I could really believe that God could fill it.

Whether it's emptiness because of a lost child, or singleness, or other lost dreams, I knew I wasn't alone. Friends around me were going through similar trials. My friend Diane was furious at God because she was still unmarried at age forty-three. Another friend was also trying to get pregnant. Another was facing an empty nest.

I was determined not to become bitter. I needed to find an answer. I pondered this question every time I dusted my dresser and moved the cameo that Kate had given me.

After a while, I wondered if my disregard for the cameo had something to do with it. At first, I laughed when I moved Mary around my dresser. *Oh, that Kate,* I thought. *Does she really think Mary could help me to have a child? To help fill this void?*

And really, underneath my disbelief was a feeling that I didn't really deserve it. Things like this *just don't happen to me!*

I looked at Mary's face in the cameo. She had believed. And she said yes.

If I had been Mary, at that moment when the angel arrived, I would have been skeptical. I would have thought, *Yeah, right. You chose me to deliver your child into the world?* And I would have found some other explanation for the archangel's message. Maybe I was having a dream, or maybe a migraine with a really elaborate aura. But a visit from an angel? No way.

Mary's yes would have been my sarcastic, "Yeah, *right.*" It comes out of my believing that miracles no longer happen. That God doesn't love me enough to show up, and that I'm not good enough, anyway.

The J. B. Phillips paraphrase of Luke 1:30 says, "Do not be afraid, Mary; God loves you dearly."

I interpret this passage to mean: Fear not, Mary. Your life will not turn out as you imagined. This is not the dream you had in mind. But don't worry. I love you. You will have an abundant life.

Maybe I had been so focused on "my" idea of abundance that I wasn't open to what God wanted to give me.

Scot McKnight, in his book *The Real Mary,* writes:

> However surprising and joyous that day must have been, when Mary whispered, "May it be" to the angel Gabriel, the inner seams of Mary's life were ripped apart. We need to remember that Mary's "may it be" to Gabriel occurred months before her "I do" to Joseph. On that day Mary heard the strange news from God that she would conceive out

of wedlock as part of God's plan. For an engaged Jewish woman, that would have been a great surprise; that's not how God or Jewish law worked. And it's not how society worked either. . . . Mary's "may it be" was an act of courageous faith.[2]

I was at the University of Saint Mary of the Lake for another retreat recently. During a break I took a walk and stumbled upon a statue of Mary. Who are you, anyway? I wanted to ask her. And what do you have to do with my life?

I looked at the smooth, carved white stone. She was holding the baby Jesus up to her cheek. I lay down on a bench near the statue and looked up at the face of Mary against the bright blue sky.

I prayed to God that I would be like Mary. That I would get past my fear and disbelief that he would bring good things, fulfilling things, life-giving things into my life, even if they were not what I had in mind, even if I never became a mother in the traditional sense.

I looked at the statue, and Mary's kind face pressed against the Christ child in her arms. I know I want to be like her: believing. Open to miracles. Accepting of God's abundance. Willing to say yes. Eager to let God use me to help bring in his kingdom. Giving myself over to God's will. And trusting in God when he says, "Do not be afraid. I love you dearly."

4

The Cost of a Marriage

I don't know how I fell in love with my husband. It just happened. After all those years of dating and agonizing and being afraid of falling for the wrong guy, I dove in headfirst and married David eight months after I met him. For once, I didn't think too much about it. I didn't try to control it; I just let it happen. Maybe the timing was right. Maybe we were both tired of waiting, and maybe it was just meant to be.

I married an imperfect man who didn't necessarily have it all together. I was (and am) an imperfect woman who didn't necessarily have it all together.

And our marriage, combined with our money issues, created a perfect storm.

Many of my ideas about money and marriage roles were deeply ingrained in me. But I quickly realized that my marriage was going to look nothing like my parents' marriage.

My parents were like most couples in their generation. My father earned the money, and my mother was a stay-at-home mom during most of my childhood.

My father is a brilliant man, despite the fact that he never went college, which is something he has regretted all his life. He's a member of Mensa, the club you have to test into in order to join, a club for people with high IQs. He's that smart.

His mother, my grandmother Mabel, died before I was born, but I heard that she was very smart too. She was a schoolteacher before she eloped with my grandfather. She taught school in a one-room schoolhouse in Iowa, and in those days, schoolteachers could not be married. She and my grandfather (a successful farmer who owned hundreds of acres of land by the time he died) kept their marriage a secret so that she could keep teaching.

Despite the lack of education, my father did very well financially. He became a real estate agent in the 1960s and soon worked his way up to become a vice president and general manager of the second-largest real estate company in Iowa. I remember as a child, going to visit him in his office in Des Moines. The scene could have been taken right out of *Mad Men*: businessmen in suits and skinny ties, midcentury modern furniture, floor-to-ceiling windows. My dad even looked the part: tall and handsome, with black hair and black-framed glasses. I felt important sitting in one of the office chairs, looking at Dad's nameplate on his desk, with the title of Vice President under it.

To impress his clients, and to haul around his growing family, he drove Cadillacs—these monstrosities that luxury cars were at that time, which probably got about two miles per gallon. But those cars were awesome. My three older sisters and I would pile our gangly arms and legs into the generous backseat of the Sedan de Ville and still have room to poke one another. My younger brother, Scott, rode in the front seat—on the pulled-down armrest between my mom and dad—like a little prince on his throne. My mom, in her beehive hairdo, sat in the passenger seat, filing her nails and turning around every now and then to settle squabbles among us four girls.

Every two years my dad would get a new Cadillac. I remember the different colors because he would contemplate for weeks what color he wanted. I remember a brown Cadillac with cream-colored leather seats, and a silver one with striped burgundy upholstery, and a tan car with deep brown interior. Dad was very picky about the colors.

And although he and my mom made many decisions together, this was one decision that was his and his alone.

We lived in our beautiful 1917 farmhouse until I was about twelve; then, after my parents got tired of that beautiful old farmhouse with the squeaky wooden floors and constant upkeep, they sold it (sad!) and built a new brick house on some land my dad owned down the road a little bit. It was a nice house, for the late 1970s, filled with brown sculpted carpet, a dark brick fireplace, a "sunken" living room, and brown woodwork. Groovy.

In our high school, which was made up mostly of farm kids and small-town kids, we were considered well-off. My dad worked hard and was a great provider. He also never missed one of our basketball games or swimming meets. He was able to strike the delicate balance between being a successful businessman and a great dad. My mom stayed at home and kept the house—as did many women of her generation—and tried to keep all of us clothed (she sewed many of our clothes) and fed. She was a genius at knitting up gorgeous sweaters (or ponchos—remember, this was the 1970s!) to keep us warm, and sewing up identical dresses for us to wear at Christmas and Easter. In our teens, we didn't want handmade clothes anymore. But that was OK, because my mother excelled at shopping as well.

Then, when I was in high school, the recession of the 1980s hit. Similar to the current recession, housing sales pretty much stopped. Suddenly my father was given the task of closing hundreds of real estate offices around the state. He told me recently how difficult that was, but he didn't delegate it because he didn't want any of his employees to have to deal with the difficult task of laying off coworkers.

Then, suddenly, he was in the same boat. The company wasn't doing well. And my dad's boss, the owner of the company, had been grooming his son to take over for quite some time. My dad could see that with the company downsizing, there wasn't going to be room for both him and the boss's son in the organizational chart. At some point, the boss's son would be ready to take over as VP. So Dad knew he had to leave. He decided to start his own real estate company—a daunting task in a down economy.

I remember those hard times for my family. We didn't get many gifts at Christmas that year, and suddenly our secure financial position felt less secure. We didn't ride in big Cadillacs anymore after my dad downsized to a compact Nissan. My father sheltered us from most of his worries. He brooded alone, not even telling our mother about the finances (it's no surprise that he had to have heart bypass surgery a few years later), but I still remember how tense and worried my parents were during that time. And I remember suddenly feeling not so rich. In fact, we felt a little bit poor.

My mom couldn't just go out and buy us new clothes at the drop of a hat. We had to "make do." And with two daughters already in college and the last three children in high school, there was always tension about who was getting what share of the limited resources. For a few years, asking for new clothes or new shoes or a better haircut made me feel guilty, because I knew my parents were feeling anxious about money.

As daughter number four, I tended to feel that I got the short end of the deal. I ended up wearing my sisters' hand-me-downs. A lot. That's embarrassing for a high-school student who wants to wear the latest fashions so that she can fit in. And it's also complicated for a girl who had a terrible body image and used wearing the right outfits to make her feel more attractive and accepted.

But soon my dad started his own real estate company, and the recession eased, and things became more stable.

But that sense of scarcity, of not having enough, stuck with me. I always felt that I was competing for my share of the pie; when I did ask for things, I expected the answer to be "we can't afford it."

Looking back, I also realize that there were mixed messages about money. We had to cut back and not spend money when my dad was laid off. But at the same time, during most of my childhood, my mom shopped a lot.

She would drag us to Younkers, the big department store in downtown Des Moines, and my brother, Scott, and I would hide underneath the big round clothes racks. I could smell the new fabric and feel the textures on my cheeks. We'd wait while mom would buy clothes for herself or for us or purchase something for the house. A new bedspread, a lampshade, a throw pillow.

In fact, there wasn't a word for it back then, but I think she was a little bit of a shopaholic. She used shopping to make herself feel better. It was probably an escape, a distraction from the stress of raising five kids.

So my dad was really good at making money, and my mom was really good at spending it. We sometimes didn't have a lot of money to spend, so we had to cut back. But that was hard to do when we were learning from my mother that buying things made you feel better.

I also learned from my parents that the husband is the one who is good at making money and providing. And that sometimes there's not enough (or it *feels* as if there's not enough) to go around, so you have to compete for the limited resources.

It's not surprising, then, looking back on all the mixed messages I got during childhood, that as an adult I ended up with money schizophrenia. And all my money anxieties and issues were intensified once I got married.

The night I met my husband, I was in a horrible mood. Our date was on a Thursday night. I had to drive all the way from the suburbs of Chicago to a coffee shop downtown, and after a long day of work, and a long commute, I was in no mood to go on a date. But I rushed home, reapplied my makeup, put on jeans and a nice black top, and got back into my car to make the drive. I sighed. *Another date, probably another disappointment.*

I'd been going on dates for a good part of twenty years. I had a few long-term relationships, but many times I met a guy and dated him once or twice, and then he never called back, or I had to gently break the news that I wasn't interested. The few times those dates did turn into longer dating relationships, they were filled with insecurity, doubt, and in one case, what bordered on emotional abuse. For me, dating had been torture.

During my thirties, at one point I was so anxious about financial security that I dated three accountants in a row. You'd think I would have gotten a clue that these guys were not the best fit for me, as we sat in long boring silence on dates. Not that accountants in general are boring. But I had nothing in common with these three particular accountants. One of these guys offered to balance my checkbook! Woo hoo! Another one instigated a "romantic" dinner conversation around 401(k)s.

While I wanted someone who could support me financially, many of these men were looking for a traditional wife who would mother their kids and stay home: a nice, compliant, submissive, evangelical wife. In other words, not me. I had determined by the end of my twenties that I was an egalitarian when it came to marriage. I wanted an equal partner. While I longed for someone to rescue me financially and give me financial security, I couldn't picture myself in the traditional role of stay-at-home mom.

I met David McCracken—a writer, editor, guitar player, free spirit, and art critic—at a coffee shop. He was casually reading a magazine when I walked in and sat down. He had dark, spiky hair and a kind face. He wore striped socks. We started talking. I can't remember what we talked about, but I do remember that I liked him within five minutes of meeting him. He seemed nice, and genuine.

We talked for three hours. He bought me more coffee. We took a walk down the street, and then we said good-bye. He took my hand in his warm hand and told me what a nice time he had had. Could he see me again? Sure, I said.

By the time I got back home, he had sent me an e-mail telling me how much he had enjoyed our date and would I like to go to a play next weekend?

I said yes.

So the next weekend, we went out again, this time to a one-woman show at an experimental theater, and then out for dinner. Sitting in the outdoor patio of the restaurant, I looked across the table at him. I still was a bit wary. He wasn't the typically church-y kind of guy I was accustomed to dating, and he looked different from the guy I had pictured as my future husband. But he was really interesting, and we had so much to talk about (not 401(k)s, although looking back, I realize maybe that wouldn't have been a bad idea).

After dinner, David walked me back to my car (we had met at the theater). Before I reached for the car-door handle, he put his arm around my waist, turned me around to face him, and before I could even think about what was happening, planted a kiss on my lips.

Wow, I thought. I was a little surprised. He just stood there, grinning. I wasn't used to a guy being that forward.

"I want to see you again," he said.

"OK."

I got home, and for the next few days, I couldn't stop thinking about that kiss.

I can't remember our third date, but by that time, we were pretty much spending time together every day. He came over after work, or I would go to his place. We went to a concert in Grant Park, and he took me sailing on his friend Dan's sailboat.

Three months later, we were engaged. And five months after that, we were married.

When we got married in May of 2005, I was working in a job I didn't like that much, writing copy for the marketing department of a large corporation. It was killing my soul to make the commute and then sit in a cubicle for eight hours every day. David was doing contract editing work for an online travel website. He made decent money—we both made about the same annual salary—but he, too, despised his job.

He was also thinking about going back to school to change careers; in fact, he'd been considering that for a long time.

Of course, I hadn't thought too much about all this before we got married. We were in love! He was gainfully employed. We had stimulating conversations (he read *The New Yorker* and Anne Lamott—woo hoo!), and he was the kindest man I had ever met.

But a few months after we were married, I started seeing the reality of the situation. Our window for having children was short; we had to try *now* if we were ever going to have kids, and even then the chances were iffy. We weren't getting any younger, so if David wanted to go back to school to change careers, he had to do it—now. How would we swing both of us changing jobs (and in his case, a whole career) if we had a baby? Who would stay home to take care of said baby? If neither of us could stay at home, how would we afford childcare? Plus, we had this debt to pay off. And we couldn't put off any of these decisions.

David applied to go back to school for the autumn of 2007. After he was accepted into the program, they called to offer him a scholarship. We saw this as a sign that he was moving in the right direction.

When he decided to go back to school, we had counted on him continuing his lucrative contracting work with the travel website. It paid well, and he worked only about twenty hours per week. While it would be difficult for him to go back to school full-time while working that much, it was doable.

But late that summer, before David started school, he found out that his contract with the website was ending. They had decided not to use contract workers anymore, handing all of their work to full-time employees. David found another freelance gig editing a website, but at a third of the pay he had been receiving.

By that time, I had left the corporate world to freelance, but without David's lucrative editing gig, and with him going back to school, we realized I needed a full-time job again. So when one of my freelance clients offered me a full-time job. I took it. Suddenly, I was making three times more money than David was.

I had never pictured myself in this situation. I had dated accountants to ensure financial stability. Now our money situation was in constant flux. Financially secure, we were not.

Despite all our financial anxiety, a year into David's master's program, as crazy as it sounds, we started thinking about adoption again. We were running out of time, and if we didn't do it soon, the window would be closed. So, in the fall of 2008, about a year after our dismal meeting with the Evil Adoption Counselor, we had Thanksgiving dinner at a friend's house. She had also invited a couple who had adopted a young girl from Russia a few years earlier. We were delighted in their daughter, who was very precocious and charming. We started talking to them about our sad attempt at adoption and told them about our experience with the adoption counselor.

"Oh, we tried that adoption agency too!" said Dana, the wife of the couple. "We had a *horrible* experience! They made us feel so awful about ourselves!"

"Really?" I said. "You mean it wasn't just us?"

"Oh, no," said Dana. "We know several people who have had bad experiences there. They want people only from the North Shore who have millions in the bank. I don't know what their problem is, but we changed to Adoption Agency X and had a great experience. You should check them out."

David and I left our friend's house in a daze. "You mean I've been feeling all of this shame for the past year," I said, "and come to find out it had nothing to do with us and our ability to be parents—it was this Evil Adoption Agency?"

I felt a huge burden of shame lifting off my back.

"Maybe we should try again," David said.

Within a year—probably before we were even matched with a child—David would be out of school. I had a decent job with a good salary. We thought we were in a good position to try again.

I made a few phone calls and got names of other adoption agencies we could check out. We finally settled on one that our friends Jane and Andy had used for their adoption. They spoke highly of Laura, the social worker who had helped with their adoption.

One day, I mustered up the courage to call Laura and tell her our situation.

"We have some debt, and my husband is in school," I told her frankly. "Do you think we're candidates for adoption?"

Laura talked with me for forty-five minutes and kindly explained the current landscape of international adoption. Instead of judging us, she seemed truly to want to help us find some solutions. She thought we could pass a home study and that we'd be good candidates for adoptive parents. She also told us that international adoption requirements had changed a lot in the past several years. We made plenty of money. So our salaries were not an issue.

The problem, she said, may be the small amount of debt we had. The USCIS (the United States Citizen and Immigration Service) would have to approve us for adoption. They had been cracking down on adoption, being much more strict about prospective adoptive parents' debt-to-income ratio, net worth, and so on.

She suggested we wait a few more months and try to pay off the rest of our credit-card debt; then David would be almost through school, and we'd be in a much better position.

I thanked her for her time and hung up the phone. I sighed deeply and felt a little stirring in my soul again. Maybe this was going to be possible after all. Maybe our adoption dream was not yet dead.

A few months later, we were closer to having our debt paid off, and David was just six months from completing school. I felt more and more confident that we could start our adoption home study again. Maybe we just needed to step out in faith and see how God would provide.

You hear of people praying about something and—voila!—a check arrives in the mail. In fact, my sister had prayed when she was adopting her daughter, Ellie. One day she was at her wits' end, not knowing how they would pay an upcoming fee for their adoption. She dropped to her knees in the living room and begged God for help.

Guess what? A check arrived in the mail the next day. I kid you not.

But remember, *things like this just don't happen to me.*

Then I thought, maybe I just lacked faith. That's it! God really wants us to adopt, but he wants us to trust him to provide.

I tried to unlock the secret to getting God to respond to my requests and treat me as specially as he had treated my sister by sending a check in the mail.

I thought I would give God a little help.

We would need around $30,000 to pay for the adoption. Not many of the adoptive parents I talked to or followed on adoption blogs had that much money in the bank. Many of them had held adoption fund-raisers to help with some of the expenses.

So we decided to get the ball rolling again by having a fund-raising concert. We'd gather our friends together. Many had volunteered to perform. They wanted to help us raise money for the adoption. Our friends John and Celeste did a short performance of a Harold Pinter play. The Nordic choir I was in performed three numbers. We had a silent auction. Another friend, an opera singer, performed. It was a smashing success, and we raised $5,000 for our adoption fund.

It was a wonderful night of gathering with friends and family. We were rolling again. We could just feel it! The adoption was becoming more and more a reality.

But it was too good to be true. Two months later, I lost my job.

Without income, there was no way we would pass a home study. Our adoption was on hold, again.

Everything seemed to be falling apart, and I feared that our marriage would, too.

I struggled to interpret and deal with this series of circumstances: the recession, David's loss of contract work, my layoff, our miscarriage, the failed adoption attempts.

Then I began to ask difficult questions. Why had David waited until we got married to change careers? Why hadn't he gone back to school years ago, when he first decided that's what he wanted to do with his life? And why wasn't he providing for me as my father had? What was *wrong* with him!

As the recession, my unemployment, David's schooling, and our money troubles went on, my resentment became more pronounced. I often slept on the couch. I stomped around our small two-bedroom condo blaming David for our situation. I lay awake at night, my mind spinning.

If he hadn't gone back to school, we'd have an adopted child by now, I kept thinking. My resentment dripped out of every pore. And the more I resented him, the more paralyzed he became.

One day I was stomping around our condo in a bad mood, thinking about a day filled with looking for work, sending out résumés, and making phone calls. David was in the bedroom getting ready to go to school. I realized he was being very quiet, and I walked into the bedroom to see why he wasn't out the door and on his way to class already.

I found him sitting on the bed, his head in his hands, looking at the floor.

"Don't you need to get ready for school?" I asked, annoyed. "What time's your class?"

He didn't say anything.

"What's wrong? Why aren't you answering me?!" I asked.

Slowly, he looked up. "You know, maybe I should just forget about school and try to find a job that pays a lot of money. I'm just dragging you down. It would be easier for us to adopt if I wasn't in school."

I sighed, and walked over to sit down next to him.

I had to be honest with myself; at times I had those thoughts. If only he weren't going back to school. If only he had a job that paid more money. Maybe I should have married one of those accountants.

Our arms were touching, and I could feel the warmth of his skin on mine.

All of a sudden, I realized how ugly I was being. The stomping, the resentment, my insistence on financial security. What was I doing to our marriage?

I wanted to be a parent—but I wanted to be a parent with David. And I wanted him to be happy in his career. I knew he wasn't the type of person who could exist in a soul-crushing job for the rest of his life. He needed to pursue his passions. And his passion was to help people with addiction and mental illness, the people on the fringes of society. I loved him for that. His compassion and kindness were two of the many things I loved about him.

Before we got married, I had dated men who made a lot of money. I remember once going out with a good-looking guy who attended my church. After the service one Sunday night, we walked down the street with a group of friends to get pizza. As we crossed an intersection, a somewhat young homeless man came up to us and asked for money.

My cute date turned to him and yelled, "Go out and get a job and stop bothering us!" I was taken aback by his blunt words and lack of compassion. And needless to say, he suddenly became less attractive to me. I mentally crossed him off my list of "guys I could marry."

I thought of that incident now, as I was remembering why I had married David. I had married him because I liked his compassion for other people and his kindness and his lack of interest in material wealth.

"Marriage is not a lifelong attraction of two individuals to each other," says Henri Nouwen, "but a call for two people to witness together God's love. The basis of marriage is not mutual affection, or feelings, or emotions and passions that we associate with love, but a vocation, a being elected to build together a house for God in this world, to be like the two cherubs whose outstretched wings sheltered the Ark of the Covenant and created a space where Yahweh could be present. Marriage is a relationship in which a man and a woman protect and nurture the inner sanctum within and between them and witness to that by the way in which they love each other."[3]

The Catechism of the Catholic Church defines the sacraments as "efficacious signs of grace, instituted by Christ and entrusted to the Church, by which divine life is dispensed to us."

Growing up Baptist, I didn't hear much about sacraments. Baptists use the word *ordinance*, which sounds more like a banal bureaucratic procedure, and over Baptist history, they whittled the list down from the Catholic seven sacraments to the Baptist two ordinances: The Lord's Supper and Baptism.

Baptism and The Lord's Supper became symbolic, not mysterious and filled with the presence of the sacred. And, as ordinances and symbols, they lost the mystery.

I like what Terry, the director of adult spiritual formation at my church says about sacraments. He says that the Catholic Church comes down to this: grace, mediation, and sacrament.

Loosely translated, that means that the church is a conduit of God's grace. Sacrament is derived from the word *sacred*, which means "God is here." There are the Big-S sacraments that the church has turned into rituals: baptism, confirmation, communion, confession, marriage, anointing of the sick, and holy orders. But then there are the small-s sacraments, which are present whenever we experience God's grace or are the mediator of God's grace to someone else.

I heard that the sacrament of marriage means being a mediator of God's grace to your spouse. "I love you no matter what," I said to David, as we sat on the bed that day. "I want you to finish school. We'll figure out the rest."

In June of 2009, David graduated from Northwestern University with an MA in counseling/psychology. It was a sunny, early summer day, and a large crowd filled the Millar Chapel on campus to watch the graduates of Northwestern's Family Institute march up the aisle to receive their diplomas. I sat in the chapel and looked at the streams of sunlight coming in through the gorgeous stained-glass windows.

The crowd stood up as the graduates marched in wearing their robes and tasseled caps. First the professors, and then the graduate students. I craned my neck to see David. Finally, he marched in, his head held high.

This had been his dream for more than ten years. It was only after we got married that he finally felt the urgency to go ahead and take the plunge to change careers. When we'd had dinner with his supervisor a month earlier, the supervisor looked at me and said, "You do know how good he is at this, don't you?"

I got a lump in my throat.

At that moment, it was all worth it—the financial insecurity, the doubts, and the struggles to understand why we were putting him through school. I knew it was the right thing, just to see him finally complete a degree that would give him more options and let him do what he really wanted to do: help people who struggled with addiction and mental illness.

Grace. Mediation. Sacrament.

After the ceremony, we took photos and documented the day. We had a party to celebrate, and friends came over. I looked at David with his kind eyes; he looked so happy. Later that day, he was going to meet a friend from church for coffee because this friend was struggling with unemployment and alcohol addiction. And later in the week he was starting a job at a community mental health clinic. It had been a long two years of unemployment and finishing school. But we had made it through. God was here.

5

Help Me to See

Never lose an opportunity of seeing anything beautiful, for beauty is God's handwriting.

—Ralph Waldo Emerson

Having eyes, do you not see? . . . And do you not remember . . .?

—Mark 8:18.

My friend Stephen is legally blind. He's also an artist—of paintings, drawings, and installations.

He wasn't always blind. Several years ago, something went awry neurologically. His doctors at the time thought it might be multiple sclerosis. Whatever it was, it robbed him of much of his sight.

David got to know him when they were both undergraduates at the University of Texas. Stephen went on to earn his MFA at the School of the Art Institute of Chicago. Ever since then, he's worked as an artist and teacher, despite his partial blindness. David and I often go to his exhibition openings, at least when they're not in Berlin or New York.

Stephen's work often explores the boundaries, or lack of boundaries, between art and life. It is conceptual work that is more challenging than the everyday notion of handsome pictures on the wall. Its fundamental concern is, What is art? What is not art? Often it may not even look like what we've come to think of as art. But then you sit with it and think about it, and with an intellectual nudge from the artist, it changes into something rich and strange, and also familiar, art as a reflection and embodiment of its place in the world.

Recently, David and I went to Stephen's show at the Hyde Park Art Center on the South Side of Chicago, where he talked about his work to a gathering of a dozen or so interested viewers.

His installation was difficult for me to understand at first. His art isn't easy to grasp. Stephen often explores art using non-art materials, including cardboard, wood, and oddly enough, stuff you would find in the kitchen.

Part of the installation involved a long table made of corrugated cardboard, with a cloth spread over it and what looked like spilled olive oil. Above, painted in large letters, was the recipe for paella. Another part of the installation involved a pile of rice on the floor, with spills of olive oil on the wall. Elsewhere, words were painted on the wall with drips of paint.

Stephen talked about how we incorporate "mistakes" into our lives every day, meaning perhaps that they're not mistakes at all. An artist can plan out a work, or he can approach it as an event and a process, something that unfolds in the making.

I loved how Stephen stretched and unfolded my idea of what art could be. How a blind artist taught me how to see something in an entirely new way.

I've always wanted to be a visual artist. I'm not sure I have those gifts, but something about creating visual art appeals to me. In high school I took art classes and spent most of my free hours in the art room painting. I hung out with the artists.

The year after my mother died, I took an art class at the Lillstreet Art Center in Lincoln Park. My teacher there—his name was Bob—was a kind, portly guy with a grey beard that hung down to his chest. He was quiet and thoughtful, and when we weren't painting, he would open his art books and show us paintings by Rembrandt, Van Gogh, and Cezanne, showing us how they used color and light.

"What colors do you see?" he would ask me, as I painted a bowl of fruit. He would stand behind me and stroke his long beard.

"Um, orange, red, blue," I'd say, stating the obvious.

But then he'd challenge me again, "No, look closer, what other colors do you *see*?"

I'd look closer, and then I would notice a reflection of light on the side of the apple—maybe a hint of yellow. And then I'd see a little bit of green tint in the orange. Bob, of course, would be able to point out a handful of other colors he could see in the bowl of fruit. Once he pointed it out, I could see it too.

It always amazed me what Bob could see.

As disappointments piled up in my life, I desperately wanted to see in a new way, sort of how Stephen and Bob could see.

But also I was learning that maybe my vision was impaired. Maybe I couldn't see all the colors in the apple. Maybe what didn't look like a blessing really was a blessing but I had not been seeing it. And maybe, like Stephen, I could try approaching my life as an event—not something mapped in advance but a venture with wrong turns and "mistakes" woven into a complex, meaningful piece of art.

Stephen once said that losing his sight was the best thing that ever happened to him. During the vast desert of my unemployment and my dying dream of motherhood, I wondered if I would ever look back and see these events in a positive way, or see how God could weave them into my story and create a beautiful piece of art.

I wanted what early Christian philosophers called the "Third Eye," the eye of true understanding.

Throughout my life, I had caught glimpses of what I call a "Ghost God." Here, there, when I needed to feel him most. But at this time, there was just . . . emptiness. Silence.

Maybe if I could see that God had a purpose for all our troubles, it would feel a little less painful. If I could just catch a glimpse of him, to know he was there. So far, there was no understanding or insight about what I was going through.

No good can come from this, I kept thinking.

"We're stuck."

"God has left the building."

I talked with Terry in his office one day. I was determined to get to the bottom of this. I saw so many people who had it worse off than me, who seemed to live abundantly in spite of their troubles.

"Any kind of crisis focuses your attention," said Terry. "What people report, in the face of a potential health crisis, like when the doctor says, 'You've got three to six months to live,' they often report an acute shift in the acuity of their sight. They say things like, 'I'm noticing things I haven't noticed in years. I just want to drink it in. I can't get enough.' It's almost like a hunger."

Ten years ago, I went to Mexico on vacation with a group of girlfriends to get a break from the frozen Midwest tundra. We packed our bikinis and shorts and tank tops and flew into Puerto Vallarta, the humid ocean air covering us like a warm blanket. Our bodies sighed as we walked out of the airport, melting away the winter stress, and breathed in the salty, flower-scented air.

We took a cab about an hour north, to a remote resort, driving through the green rolling hills and laughing about how our white, pasty Midwestern skin would look in our bikinis as we lay on the beach.

I knew some women in the group better than others. My friend Sara was someone I had known a long time. While she wasn't in my closest circle of friends, we saw each other often because we went to the same church, and we'd met together for lunch or coffee on several occasions. We had a lot in common. And her dry sense of humor contrasted with what my now-husband calls my "dour Swedish vibe."

That week, we spent hours on the beach and by the pool talking. We snorkeled, went whale watching, and one fatefully hilarious day, Sara, Eileen, and I tried surfing.

A twenty-something guy who worked at the resort where we were staying was nice enough to take us to a remote part of the beach. First he taught us how to stand on the surfboards, and then how to go from lying prone on the boards to getting up to our knees and then to our feet.

Surfer boy would help us, one by one, paddle out beyond where the waves were breaking, and then help us turn around and paddle toward shore as the waves came behind us. We were supposed to push ourselves up from the prone position to the kneeling position, and then up to a standing position. Sounds simple, but we were out of shape, and our arms were tired from paddling. So pushing our late-thirty-something bodies up to a standing position was next to impossible.

Watching each of us attempt to get up on the surfboards gave Sara plenty of fodder for her sarcastic quips, and we couldn't stop laughing. Our cute surfer boy got a little exasperated with us. Before we left the beach, Sara asked him to take a picture of us standing on our boards on the sand. In the photo, we're poised for the drop into the curl, tan and happy, laughing at Sara's commentary. I'll never forget that day.

After seven days of ocean bliss, we packed up our salt- and sand-encrusted bikinis and boarded a plane back to Chicago—relaxed, tan, and filled with good memories of long girl-friend talks, surfing, kayaking, whale watching, and reading.

A few months later, I was in my apartment when the phone rang. It was my friend Val. "Did you hear about Sara?" she asked.

"No. What's up?"

"Sara has breast cancer."

"Oh, that's so sad!" I replied. To be honest, I didn't have much of a reaction. Val was close to another woman named Sara, who I didn't know well at the time. While I was sad about the news, I thought she was calling me to tell me about that Sara.

But then it slowly dawned on me. "Wait—which Sara are you talking about?"

Then, as she confirmed it was our mutual friend Sara—the wise-cracker on our Mexico trip—my heart sank into my stomach.

"They found two lumps in her breast. It doesn't look good."

I hadn't seen Sara in a few months; we had both been busy with work and life in general. I was having a hard time getting my head around this news. Sara was still in her thirties. She was much too young to get breast cancer. We had just been in Mexico surfing, for Pete's sake! She was so healthy and vibrant, and alive.

The cancer may have already been growing in her body that day we laughed hysterically on our surfboards. Things like that aren't supposed to happen to someone in her thirties.

Slowly, over the next few weeks, we heard that the cancer had spread. She had surgery, then chemotherapy. I met her for lunch after her treatments had started and she was wearing a wig. I didn't know what to expect because I hadn't seen her for a while. But she walked up to the café looking beautiful, her porcelain skin glowing from under the bangs of her dark wig.

As we sat there in the café, we just talked about life. Before her diagnosis, when we were single and in our thirties, our conversations always drifted to dating, jobs, clothes. Now we talked about treat-ment, losing her hair, her prognosis, and how she was dealing with the scary prospect of her cancer coming back or spreading.

As we talked, she moved her arms and winced. "Ouch," she said, and touched her hand to the middle of her chest.

"What's wrong," I asked.

"Oh, I've had this pain in my chest for a few weeks. My doctors checked it out and just think it's a pulled muscle."

Sara and I lingered over lunch, and she gave me a big hug when we left, both of us promising that we'd get together again soon.

A few months later, I heard through the grapevine that the pain in her chest was actually the cancer that had settled into her bones. The cancer had spread, and Sara's prognosis had suddenly become much more grim.

In the midst of all of this, I attended her fortieth birthday party—which was a huge, bittersweet celebration of Sara's life. And at that party, Sara met someone. A man who had been attending our church for years had come to the party, and although Sara had known him as an acquaintance for a long time, at the party they started talking. Something just clicked, and over the next few months, they fell in love.

Sara wasn't sure she trusted the relationship; she didn't just want to be someone's charity case. But he assured her that, no, he was honestly, truly in love with her, no matter what happened.

From the time of our trip to Mexico to the time Sara was in the end stages of her illness, about three years passed. During this time, I had also met, and married, David. When Sara got married—ten months before she died—she borrowed my wedding shoes. When I dropped them off, we sat in her living room and talked. She had no hair; whole-brain radiation for the treatment of brain tumors had killed off the last follicles. She would never grow hair on her head again. But she didn't care. She looked beautiful that day.

She told me she wanted her wedding to be a celebration of how, in the midst of suffering, there could be joy and happiness. To show people that God is found in the midst of pain.

Sara and her husband walked down the aisle, after the ceremony, to the song "O Happy Day."

I didn't visit Sara very often during the last three months of her life. I wanted to keep enough distance so that her family, husband, and closest friends could be with her in her final days. But a few months before she died, she e-mailed me. "Hey, do you want to get together?"

I hadn't seen her for about a month, and I was shocked when I saw her walk out to meet me. Her clothes hung off her thin limbs, and she had a scarf wrapped around her head. Her skin was sort of an ashy yellow, and she walked slowly. But as she approached the car, she smiled, and I saw the sarcastic, funny, Sara I had always known.

We drove to a little sushi place, and I felt a little awkward and afraid. How do you talk to someone who is dying? What do you say? Do you talk about the past? Do you acknowledge her weight loss and physical decline? Or do you just talk normally, like two girlfriends getting caught up? But Sara seemed calm and peaceful. She asked about me, and David, and we talked about marriage. She told me what her first months of marriage were like. How she liked to cook for her new husband. About the puppy they just got from the shelter. I think she could sense my awkwardness and countered it with warmth and understanding.

Soon I felt at ease but got the sense that while Sara appeared present, she also seemed far away. During the conversation, she seemed very focused on tiny details of the objects on the table, things I would have overlooked or ignored. The shape of the bowl. How the tea leaves in the bottom of her tea cup formed a beautiful design. The color of the bamboo tray that held our sushi.

She moved in slow motion, and barely touched her food. She appeared to be letting go of this physical world, and in doing so, seeing things that most people would never notice. It was as if she were lovingly looking and taking mental pictures of this physical place she had called home for forty years, much as a parent memorizes and studies that face of a child before he gets in the car to go off to college. I sensed that, as she was letting go of this world, little by little, she was noticing things that before she wouldn't have seen. Seeing beauty in the tiny tea leaves.

After dinner, I dropped off Sara at her condo building. I gave her a hug, and then she got out of the car and I watched her shuffle into the building. I would never see her again. I later realized that she had asked me to dinner to say good-bye.

The last few months of Sara's life, a large tumor spread from her liver toward her lungs. Her liver started failing; fluids swelled her legs and torso. *Let this cup pass from me*, I'm sure she thought in those last excruciating months. But I'm also sure Sara had a peace that only God can give.

I was in the Volkswagen dealership getting my Jetta worked on and drinking the dreadful complimentary coffee when I got a call on my cell phone from another friend, Jen, telling me that Sara had died that morning. I walked outside when I answered the call, so when Jen told me the news, I felt the breath go out of me. I sat down on a small patch of grass next to a tree. I felt the sun on my face and the world spinning around me.

Nicholas Wolterstorff says, "I shall look at the world through tears. Perhaps I shall see things that dry-eyed I could not see."

Here's what Sara taught me: our suffering changes us. It gives us an urgency for life that we wouldn't have otherwise. It teaches us compassion and helps us see the tea leaves. I'm not sure I like the price, but I am looking for resurrection stories now, in the midst of this suffering—my own suffering, which seems so paltry compared to what Sara went through.

How can we see more clearly? Is there a way to cultivate a way of being that gives us this heightened gratitude and appreciation, a way of seeing God in the most mundane but beautiful things in our everyday lives?

├─────────┤

I met with Laura, my spiritual director. She suggested that I look back and try to see where God had shown up in my past experiences. Maybe that would help in my current situation.

I have a hard time sitting still and being quiet. Although I didn't do it every day, I tried to go through that scrapbook of memory.

At first, I didn't come up with much, thinking back on my somewhat lonely childhood, long years of being single, my seemingly dying dream of being a mother, having our adoption put on hold, and our struggles with money.

I went to my actual scrapbook and got out some old photos. One photo was from my first birthday. Now, because I was daughter number four, there aren't many baby photos of me. The whole novelty of having a daughter was, by this time, wearing thin for my parents, or so I suppose. So this was one of just a few photos I have of me, not counting the usual gawky grade-school pictures.

I stared at this photo for a long time.

While I grew up in a loving home, we weren't perfect. My parents did their best at making us all feel loved. But for whatever reason, I remember some parts of my childhood as being lonely. The story I've always told myself is that since I was the fourth girl and my parents wanted a boy, I was unwanted. I was also born four months after my grandmother died, so I was born into a family in the midst of grief. I remembered feeling lost in the shuffle, ignored because I was the youngest and quietest.

But this photo told a different story. I am sitting in a high chair, and my sister Ann is holding a birthday cake, and she has a huge smile on her face. My oldest sister, Amy, always the protective one, has her arm around the back of the high chair. She, too, has a big smile on her face. And my sister Sara is standing off to the side. She's only three at the time, but she's grinning as well. We're all dressed in fancy dresses to celebrate my birthday. And my mother is standing behind us, her arms around Amy and Ann, beaming at the camera.

Well, that's funny, I thought. *This doesn't look like the picture of a child who is unwanted.* I am surrounded by siblings excited by the existence of a little sister, and a woman who seems proud to be the mother of these four little girls.

Maybe God was there after all, I thought, loving me through my sisters and father and mother.

I thought of those long years in my twenties and thirties when I was single. During that time, my life was filled with a group of loving friends and adventures such as working in an orphanage in Kosovo and trips to Mexico and Hawaii with my girl-friends—adventures I wouldn't have had if I had been married with children.

And I realized how much I had grown emotionally and spiritually during the lonely times of my singleness.

Then I thought back on the past few years, since I had got married, and about our long struggle to become parents, to settle in our careers and become financially stable.

I thought about how David and I have grown closer together in the struggle. I remembered the look on his face when he earned his master's degree. And how, after a scary job loss, I ended up in a job I like ten times better than my previous one. I remembered when I have had to totally trust that God's timing might be better than mine. I've had to let go of control. And then I realized how much I had grown and changed.

Maybe God was there after all.

I was seeing the Ghost God in the Polaroids of my life—there, in the background, showing up in ways I had never realized.

Maybe God was here with me now, too, even though I couldn't see him clearly. Maybe he was lurking in the shadows, waiting to be found in a Polaroid picture sometime in the future.

As I contemplated all these things, I slowly became more aware of everything around me.

I started noticing small things, beautiful things. I started being grateful for a sunny day. Or the way the moon glowed over the city on my walk to the train in the evening. I started seeing God in conversations I had with hurting friends, or in chance encounters that began to feel like something other than random. "Ghost God" was showing up. Or I was getting better at seeing him. I was seeing beauty everywhere, even in the ugliest places. I wasn't dying of cancer. But in some ways I *was* dying, was being forced to let go of so many things.

I thought once again of the movie *A Serious Man.* There's a scene in which Larry Gopnik, the main character, is standing in an L.A. parking lot with an acquaintance, Carlos, and they're both looking out onto a valley filled with smog. The sky is brown and thick. But as the sun sets, the sky turns a brilliant orange, and Carlos says, "Sometimes awful things have their own kind of beauty."

The Hebrew word for seeing actually means "experiencing."

I was slowly beginning to understand that abundance had something to do with this third eye. Seeing had to do with feeling the profound joy and sadness of life. It had to do with being alive—and awake.

One day, on my walk to the train I take to work, I stopped in the middle of the sidewalk. It was an early spring day, and the trees were still bare. The sky was cloudy. A dull, depressing pall had covered the city for weeks, and we thought spring would never come. But that day, on a bare tree next to a gray house, a brilliant red cardinal was singing.

It was a spot of crimson in the midst of bleakness. Those who do not live in Chicago or other northern cities might not understand the beauty of a single bright-red cardinal after a brutal, dark winter. It is a message: *There is hope! Spring is coming, even though you may not believe it.* Even though it seems that it will *never* come.

I stood there for about five minutes. As people walked by, I pointed and said, "Do you see that?!" Busy commuters paused and looked. They nodded at me and walked by. They probably thought I was a little wacky. But I didn't care. I was too in awe of the brilliance of the red, the beauty of the cardinal's song in the silent morning, the contrast of the red and the gray, bare branches, the cold wind on my face. "Do you see that?" I kept saying.

Do you *see?*

6
Can't Let Go of This Dream

By the fall of 2010, David and I had been working in new jobs for about a year. We had paid off some of the additional debt that had accumulated when I was laid off. We felt a little more financially secure. We had that $5,000 in our adoption account from our fundraising concert.

While we still had some debt, we didn't have time to wait until it was all paid off to try to adopt again. We weren't getting any younger. Like so much of our marriage, we didn't have much time. The clock was ticking.

It was now or never, and this was probably our last chance.

"Do you think we should just forget about it?" I asked David. "Maybe we should just be one of those childless couples who travels around and has a carefree life."

We thought about it. Prayed about it. We just couldn't shake the feeling that our family was meant to be more than just the two of us. We had enough love to give a child. We had a bedroom waiting.

I don't know what being "called" to adopt means. I heard that all the time in Christian circles. "God is *calling* us to adopt from Ethiopia!" someone will exclaim.

If being called means not being able to stop thinking about it, or reading blogs about it, or feeling as if your life isn't complete without it, then we felt called.

We tried, again, to adopt. I called Laura, the nice adoption counselor, and she assigned us to her colleague Lily for our adoption home study.

73

We liked Lily immediately. She was young and positive and didn't seem judgmental of our situation. I had sent her our financial worksheet before we started the home study, just to make sure we would pass. "I think we're okay to move forward," she said. "We may need some more documentation down the road, but I think we're good for now."

We met with Lily for our interviews. David met with her separately; then she interviewed me, and then the two of us together. We attended a daylong international-adoption seminar. We filled out forms, got our fingerprints taken, filled out more forms. Got physical exams. The paperwork was overwhelming.

The whole process took four months. During that time, we got some discouraging news: Ethiopia was now requiring adoptive parents to take two trips to the country. One trip was to attend a court meeting and to meet the child—which would help ensure that adoption agencies and orphanages weren't trying to do a "bait and switch" with the child (giving information about one child, only to offer another child to the adoptive parent later). The second trip was to pick up the child.

The two-trip rule would add even more expense to an already expensive adoption. Plus, it meant we would have to take more time off from work.

Then we discovered, a few months later, that Ethiopia was slowing down international adoptions by 90 percent, to give their in-country officials more time to scrutinize the paperwork of the children—that is, to make certain they were truly orphans and not children taken from families or otherwise bought and sold through a black-market system.

While these measures were certainly understandable to protect the children, it also meant that more kids would remain in orphanages for longer periods of time. The true orphans might linger in orphanages until they aged out, only to end up trying to fend for themselves on the streets of Addis Ababa.

For us, it meant that the wait times to be matched with a child and then wait for the paperwork to go through court could become much longer. We were too old to wait three years for a child. At the rate we were going, we'd have to check out of the retirement village in order to see our child graduate from high school.

Apparently we weren't the only ones struggling to jump through all the hurdles to adoption internationally. According to the State Department, international adoptions have declined by 60 percent since 2004 because of the more complicated process and the longer wait times.

I talked to Lily, and she convinced me that we should continue moving forward, because with international adoption, things were always in flux and the wait times might not stay high for very long.

So, we moved ahead. But there was another hurdle that proved to be insurmountable.

During the last interview with Lily, when we were almost done with the paperwork, she started asking questions. "How would you come up with the $30,000 to pay for the adoption?"

"Well, we're planning, once we pass the home study, to apply for adoption grants, maybe take a loan from my 401(K), and try to pay the fees as we go," I said. Plus, we had the $5,000 in savings.

My sisters had done something similar. For most adoptions, fees aren't due all at once. First, there's the home study fee of around $2,000. Then the international agency fee, which could be around $8,000. Then the dossier fee, travel fees, and so on.

I felt confident we could scrape together the money when we needed it.

"Well, I'm afraid U.S. Citizenship and Immigration Services is going to require you to document, up front, how you're going to pay for the entire adoption," she said.

"What?! I thought you told us that our financials looked fine. Are you telling us that we may not pass the home study unless we can show we have $30,000 in the bank?"

"Well," said sweet Lily, who was seeming less sweet by the minute, "I recently had a couple who has a similar financial situation as you do, and USCIS required them to document, up front, how they would pay for their adoption. So they had to show how they were going to take an equity loan from their mortgage. And it's not good enough just to tell USCIS that you'll try to apply for adoption grants."

My heart sank. With the downturn in the economy, I knew the equity we had in our condo had plummeted; we could not take out an equity loan. Our parents were all in ill health, and the economy had hit their finances, too. We couldn't ask them for money, no matter how much they might want to help us. I had already borrowed so much money from my 401(k) to keep us going during my layoff that it was on life support.

We could probably come up with part of the money, but not all $30,000. Not all at once. I felt sick.

We're going to have to figure this out, we told Lilly. We'll get back to you.

In the following week, we thought of all our options. How would we come up with all $30,000? Right now?

Slowly, the realization hit: we had no more options.

We had already scrimped and cut back in all areas of our finances to pay off our debt. David and I were in a constant state of stress in our marriage. We were trying to stick with a budget. It was helping, but it left us feeling resentful of each other and stressed about paying off debt and saving. We hadn't been on a vacation in two years. David was working three jobs—his therapy practice and two online editing jobs. I was commuting to my job downtown and freelancing on the side.

In some ways, the recession was putting the last nail in the coffin of our dream. I kept thinking: *if only we still had equity in our condo. . . . If only I hadn't gotten laid off. . . . If only David had been able to find work that paid a little bit more. . . . If only . . .*

We were at the end of our resources, both financial and otherwise. With the changing Ethiopia adoption program, and now this financial requirement, the barriers were too high.

"I can't do this anymore. It's over," I told David one afternoon soon after that, as we were sitting on the couch. He put his head in his hands and stared at the floor. The cat rubbed against his leg.

I called Lilly. "I'm afraid we're going to have to end our home study," I said. "If we're required to show USCIS that we have $30,000 in the bank now, then we can't do it."

My shame kept me from telling her how angry I was that she had given us the go ahead four months before, telling us that our "finances were fine." But instead, I once again felt unworthy, and that God was slamming the door shut.

I didn't understand. Did he not want us to be parents? If he did, I thought, then something would have worked out.

There's an ancient Chinese proverb that adoptive parents tend to quote a lot. It goes like this: An invisible red thread connects those who are destined to meet, regardless of time, place, or circumstance. The thread may stretch or tangle, but it will never break.

I had always felt warm and fuzzy when I heard it. I believed it. I believed that the child I was going to adopt was connected to me by an invisible thread, and one day we would meet and it would be as if we were meant to be together.

But this red thread that supposedly connected us had been broken, and I imagined her lying in a small cot in an orphanage somewhere in Ethiopia, waiting for us to come and get her.

We had a bedroom waiting for her. We had a doll my sister had given to me when she first learned we were going to adopt from Ethiopia. The doll is in the closet, waiting for tiny arms to embrace it at bedtime. We had so much love in our hearts for this child that we were ready to burst.

But the red thread had been broken, and we could not get to her. The hurdles were too high. The cost was too much. The red tape could not be untangled.

Then there are the heartwarming stories from Christians about adoption; Christians take to heart the command from Scripture to take care of widows and orphans.

But these heartwarming stories just make me mad, because my story does not have a heartwarming ending. I used to be that idealistic about adoption. I used to feel "called by God" to adopt (and I still do), and because of that, I thought that everything would fall into place and we would have an amazing story about how God led us to the perfect child for us.

Now I'm not so sure. I've lost faith. Because in the past four years as we've pursued Ethiopian adoption, the doors have closed—or more like, they've been slammed shut. Why would we feel "called" to do something, and yet the doors slam shut anyway? What kind of cruel joke was this?

But what happens when a couple feels "called" by God to adopt and is willing and able to face all the challenges that come with it, and yet, and yet, the doors close? The money doesn't appear. The hurdles become too overwhelming. As time goes on, they grow weary, and well, they just give up.

Do I just not have enough faith? Am I not willing enough to sacrifice?

Intellectually and spiritually I understand that sometimes "God closes a door" or that some things "just aren't meant to be." In my most trustful times, it is clear to me that maybe we will not be parents of a child from Ethiopia because of some kind of destiny. Maybe our paths will lead us elsewhere—to a place that is just as fulfilling and meaningful. Maybe the love we reserved for a child will find another place to make a difference.

But right now, I read adoption blogs, and I hear about new books that tell stories of adoption. I see families together at the beach, and I hear the neighbor children playing outside on their deck. And all I can think about is that broken red thread—the red thread that was supposed to lead me to my child.

7
Rotten Bones

A heart at peace gives life to the body, but envy rots the bones.
—Proverbs 14:30 (New International Version)

A few months after our last attempt to adopt, I was browsing Facebook, looking at status updates, and I read one from a woman I knew from my childhood.

"Peter and I want to announce some great news! We're adopting a child from Ethiopia!"

Wow, I thought. It seemed that, all around me, people were adopting children from Ethiopia, and each time I heard the news, I felt a twinge of envy.

I wonder how they can adopt on their salaries, I thought. After the financial scrutiny that we had been through, I knew it wasn't easy. Peter was a pastor of a small church, and Heather was a stay-at-home mom. I knew they probably didn't have an extra $30,000 lying around. I also thought it was a bit unfair. They already had two children. Still, this was one more loving family who would be sparing a child from life in an orphanage or on the streets, so I knew it was a good thing.

I sent her a message on Facebook: "Hey, Heather! So glad to hear you're adopting from Ethiopia! That's so exciting! David and I tried to adopt, too, but then realized we couldn't come up with the money. It's so expensive! But I hope you have better luck!"

I tried to be encouraging and chipper, despite the fact that I was burning with envy inside.

A few hours later I got a message back from Heather: "Hey, Karen. Yes, we're so excited to adopt! We can't wait! We're so thankful that an anonymous donor is financing our entire adoption! We can't believe it! It's a real answer to prayer, and God is *soooooo* good!"

I read that message and wanted to pick my laptop off the desk and hurl it at the wall.

You have to be kidding me! Seriously? Someone is giving them $30,000 for the whole adoption?! The. Whole. Thing?

I wanted to scream. I was so angry I couldn't even respond to her message.

I ranted at God. "Seriously, God? Seriously? Why them and not us? Couldn't you give us just this one thing? What, you think they'll be better parents to a little adopted child than us? And they already have kids—why do they need more?"

In response to my rant, there was silence.

Under my breath I kept saying a mantra: *I will not be bitter. . . . I will not be bitter. . . . I will not be bitter.* But it's easier said than done.

David and I were stuck in the doldrums, our sails motionless and flat—the seas like glass. On our sixth anniversary, after I asked him to look back on the past six years of our marriage, David jokingly made the comment, "We've gotten nowhere."

We both laughed at how pathetic it seemed. I knew it wasn't true; we had grown in unexpected ways and had more abundance than most people.

There was so much that had happened, but it wasn't anything that people would see on the surface of our lives. We had grown. David had finished a degree. We had developed deeper relationships; we had loved others; David had helped people in his therapy practice; we had found a spiritual community that we loved and were committed to; we were making progress on our debt. The spiritual lessons we had learned were priceless.

Maybe in a certain way, we were the ones clipping along under a strong wind and full sails on Lake Michigan on a clear blue day and those around us were stuck in the doldrums.

But I knew that by comparing my life to other people's lives, I wasn't yet totally free to live abundantly. Because it would keep me focused on what I didn't have.

If things didn't change, I would end up like Daniel Plainview in the movie *There Will Be Blood*. In a conversation with his half brother, Daniel Plainview says:

> Are you an angry man, Henry?
> Henry Brands: About what?
> Plainview: Are you envious? Do you get envious?
> Henry Brands: I don't think so. No.
> Plainview: I have a competition in me. I want no one else to succeed. I hate most people.
> Henry Brands: That part of me is gone . . . working and not succeeding—all my failures has left me. . . . I just don't . . . care.
> Plainview: Well if it's in me, it's in you. There are times when I look at people and I see nothing worth liking. I want to earn enough money I can get away from everyone.

If you've seen the movie, you'll know what an ugly, dark, angry character Daniel Plainview is. In the end, he's alone in his mansion, miserable, still filled with hatred.

Would I end up like Daniel Plainview?

That's the last thing I wanted. *I will not be bitter. . . . I will not be bitter. . . . I will not be bitter. . . .*

I thought that if I just said it enough, it would become a reality. But I needed to do more than just say a mantra. I couldn't stop being envious of friends and family. And according to Proverbs, this envy was rotting my bones.

And it was leading to despair. "I know that the fastest way to despair is by comparing one's insides with another's outsides," writes poet Max Ehrmann.

In order to avoid becoming bitter, I knew I needed to stop comparing myself with others. To be able to live in a world that seemed unfair. To love a God who seemed silent, at least when he wasn't bestowing random blessings on everyone except me. To remain in community with people who were getting things I thought I deserved and wanted.

My comparisons were ruining relationships. My envy was keeping me from seeing all the good things I had in my life, and distancing me from friendships with people whom I perceived to be getting what I wanted (which was pretty much everyone).

I also knew this was not going to be easy. I needed help. I went to talk to Terry.

"So how can I experience abundance when everyone is finding abundance but me?" I began. Terry burst out in laughter. "Ohhhh, that's the hardest thing of all!" He laughed like a jackal. I told him he was being cruel.

When people talk about abundance, Terry told me, not many tell us how to experience God's abundance when it seems like everyone else is getting what you want.

He sighed and stared at the ceiling, measuring his words carefully. While I waited, I stared at his Birkenstocks. He was wearing white socks with his Birkenstocks. He rubbed his chin as he thought.

After a few moments, he said, "What if it's all a gift?"

I wasn't sure what he meant.

"It comes down to two options: either it's all an accident, or a gift. If it's a gift, and you predicate your life on that perception, then it lends itself to a posture of trust to the author of the gift. You're going to say, 'Oh, I didn't own this anyway.'"

He went on to explain. "In our culture, we tend to say, 'this is *my* land, *my* car, *my* mortgage, *my* garden, *my* child.' What if we disciplined ourselves to not assume ownership? What if someone gave you your car, your house, your land, your oxygen, your friendships? I just think we're seduced into taking all this for granted. And not only that, but we take it further to an attitude of *I* earned or *I* deserve these things. And that's when we're offended. What if we don't deserve any of it? What if it's all a gift? Then the impulse in response to those gifts is reverence and gratitude."

I started looking at what I did have—which, honestly, was much more than most people on this planet possess. I had food in my cupboards, a roof over my head, a loving husband, a large, close family, friends, a job. I lived in a city that was full of culture and life. Really, I had so much.

But just making a list didn't seem like enough. I needed to move toward those people I envied. Otherwise, I'd end up alone and bitter, having pushed away all my friends and family who had what I wanted.

I remembered hearing about a Buddhist tradition of praying that I thought might help. We start by praying for ourselves, that we would have peace, love, grace. Then we broaden the circle to pray for our family and then our close friends, then broaden the circle even more to include our acquaintances, then the broader community, then the world.

Finally, we pray for our enemies. I guess I could say that those people I envied were my enemies.

I tried. I started praying for them. I also tried to feel happy for my friends. Fake it till you make it. But it sort of worked.

When a friend got her foot in the door to have an editor look at her book, I didn't want to be friends with her anymore. Life was like a competition, and I was forever sizing up my opponents. If one got a leg up somehow—a connection to help her get published, or a miraculous pregnancy after forty, or a big house in the burbs—I started distancing myself from that person.

I was headed quickly into a Daniel Plainview scenario.

Every time I felt competitive with someone who got a lucky break that I didn't get, instead of isolating myself and letting envy get between us, I forced myself to move toward that person. I prayed for her or him. I told her I was happy for her. I even helped friends connect with editors—when I knew it might mean that they would get a book published before I did.

It worked. Sort of. More often than not, I was at least close enough to that person (instead of observing from a distance) that I realized how hard life was for her, too.

Once, I spent the better part of a week obsessing about a friend who had gotten her manuscript placed on the desk of an editor I admired. And I was convinced that if her book was published, then mine wouldn't be. We were writing about similar things, and I was convinced there wasn't enough room in the world for both of our books.

At first I didn't want to hang out with her anymore. She was the enemy.

But then I had a pep-talk with myself. "OK, even if she gets her book published, that doesn't mean yours won't be published. *Calm down,* and remember: *She's your friend!*"

I didn't have control of the situation. I had to trust that everything would work out fine, for both of us. After all, this friend had been out of work for months. She needed a boost. It would be great if she got a book deal.

I forced myself to ask about her book. "Have you heard from the editor yet?"

"No," she told me. She was discouraged, but waiting patiently. I told her to hang in there; the editor was probably just on vacation or something.

After a while, I started sympathizing with my friend. It had been months, and she still hadn't heard from the editor.

Finally, at a dinner party, I once again asked about the book. Had she heard anything?

"Oh, yes!" she said. "And it was a definite no!" She laughed, but I could see the disappointment in her eyes.

"I'm so sorry," I told her, and I really was. (I swear I wasn't secretly pumping my fist in victory.)

We talked for a while, and instead of feeling relief or (God forbid) happiness at her misfortune, I sat with her as she told me about how hard it was to hear the editor's critique. But how she was moving on, sending the manuscript to other agents and editors. I wasn't happy about her disappointing news. I mourned with her and truly wanted her to succeed.

This never would have happened if I had been stuck in my envy and hadn't reached out to her.

I started practicing this tactic with other friends. When a friend had a baby, I'd pour out the congratulations and ask to hold the precious being. I posted congratulations messages on friends' Facebook walls if they got a book published, or found a new job, or went on a vacation.

I knew that on the surface, their lives might look great, but there was probably more to the story. Their Facebook personas probably weren't telling the whole truth.

Eric Simpson says,

> The kingdom of God is a realm of rulership wherein the walls separating us are dismantled: We become equal as human persons made

in the image of God, and the judgments of comparison, either con-
demning others through pride or ourselves through shame, are
thrown down. Jesus draws out the distinctions between the two king-
doms, whose kings vie to rule our hearts, later in the Sermon on the
Mount as recorded by Matthew. "Do not lay up for yourself treasures
on earth, where moth and rust destroy and where thieves break in
and steal, but lay up for yourselves treasures in heaven, where neither
moth nor rust destroys."[4]

I wanted to tear down the wall of envy brick by brick, to love others,
to store up treasures in heaven.

I confessed my envy to Father Pat.

This was the first time I had confessed to a priest. Like your aver-
age Protestant who doesn't see the point in confessing to a priest
(why not just go straight to God?), I was most skeptical of this sacrament. I had confessed my sins to God and asked forgiveness over and
over again in the OCD faith of my childhood. Would the Catholics
think that this was the only "confession" that counted?

But like many of my hesitancies about Catholicism, this fear was
replaced with a deeper understanding. I learned that priests don't
"forgive" you, but they confer God's grace. And rather than ask for
forgiveness alone in my prayers with God, I liked the fact that I
could articulate them to a real, live human being and have a witness.
There had to be some kind of power in that.

There were four priests available for reconciliation, and I picked
Father Pat because he was a Jesuit and he had a kind face.

"I envy people," I told him. "I mean, I envy pretty much everyone. Every single person I meet has something I think I want. And I
get this feeling that if they have it, then I can't. That God loves them
more than me."

"I see," he said, and looked at me with his kind eyes. He put his
hand on my arm. He thought for a moment. I wondered if I should

go into detail, although it would be quite embarrassing to admit how many people I envied: I envied Jane because she had three beautiful kids. I envied Alexis because she had a rich grandmother who had helped her pay off her mortgage. I envied my coworkers when they seemed to get assigned better projects than I did. I envied friends who got books published. I envied other friends who had the money to fly to Europe for vacation.

But I didn't need to explain. Father Pat understood.

"It's keeping me from having healthy friendships, and I think it's keeping me from God."

Father Pat nodded in understanding. "These things you say you think you want, these things you think everyone else has and you don't—do you think that's really what you want?"

I looked at him, a little confused. *Of course I want them,* I thought. *That's why I'm envious!*

"Do you think all these things that other people have—children, published books, a house, more money—do you think those are the things that you're really longing for?"

At that point, he starting talking about St. Ignatius, and our desires, and how St. Ignatius says that there are desires underneath our desires. He kept talking, and it was all a blur because I was nervous and didn't know what I was supposed to do, and I saw his lips moving but was lost in my own thoughts. But then this question broke through: "So what do you *really* want?"

When he finished talking, I blurted. "I think what I really want is to know that God loves me." I started crying. "I know it in my head, but I can't seem to feel it. I don't really believe that God loves me!"

He looked at me with his Jesuit-kind eyes again and gave me my "penance." "Well, that's what you need to do: you need to pray again and again that you feel God's love."

Then he prayed for me, that I would feel God's forgiveness and love deep in my bones.

That was it. I thought maybe I should say some Hail Marys or go around confessing my envy to all those people I envied. *It has to be harder than this,* I thought. I wanted some penance to absolve me of all of my ugliness, to rid me of what poet Anne Sexton calls the "rat inside of me."

But no. Father Pat knew what I needed. I put my hand over his and said, "Thank you, Father." He smiled.

And then I turned and walked down the marble steps of the chapel.

8

Blessed Are the Poor

Our life of poverty is as necessary as the work itself. Only in heaven will we see how much we owe to the poor for helping us to love God better because of them.

—Mother Teresa

It's God's will for you to live in prosperity instead of poverty. It's God's will for you to pay your bills and not be in debt.

—Joel Osteen

David and I once went to a daylong financial workshop at a well-known megachurch in the Chicago suburbs. It took us an hour to drive there. We sat in a room filled with suburbanites dressed in pricy jeans or khakis and golf shirts.

"What did you get me into!" David whispered, a little desperately, as he looked around at the earnest faces. We felt a little out of place in our urban-black clothes and boots. Plus, we had brought a little cynicism to the suburbs with us. Not ones to like platitudes, easy answers, or anything that's too mainstream, we were like the immature, adult equivalents of those kids in high school who sit in the back row of the classroom and tip their chairs against the wall to take a nap during class. We were the freaks and geeks in a room full of cheerleaders and captains of the football team.

"Just try to stay open-minded," I whispered back. "What do we have to lose?"

We were trying to recover from almost nine months of unemployment. We needed all the financial advice we could get. I was a little addicted to reading books by Suze Orman and Dave Ramsey. This was another attempt at finding financial salvation.

I was thankful for recently having been offered a contract job at a small marketing agency. I liked the people, the work, and the pay. I was hoping that the job would turn into something permanent. David was also working two part-time jobs. In the scheme of things, I knew we were very fortunate. I kept reading stories of people who were still struggling to find work, trying to survive on unemployment.

But getting jobs was just the beginning of a long journey. The bleeding had stopped, but now, if the work continued to come, it would be months, or years, before our financial wounds would heal.

My contract was to last for three months. I hoped it would stretch longer. But I was afraid to hope. I just put my head down and worked. I was afraid that it wouldn't last, that they would decide they didn't need me after all, that some other shoe would drop. I think I was suffering the recession's version of post-traumatic stress disorder.

So at the financial seminar, we settled into our metal folding chairs and tried our best to listen to the speaker.

As a group, we went through the workbook we had received at the beginning of the day. The speaker, one of the church leaders who had a degree in finance, was clean-cut, wore khakis and a button-down shirt, and seemed kind. *I bet he's been sticking to a budget since he was five,* I thought.

The kind, clean-cut man talked about our attitudes about money. Apparently we all have a "money personality." Having money means different things to different people. What was our money personality? the speaker asked? What does money mean to you? Security? Freedom? Power? The ability to be generous? Comfort?

"All of the above!" I wrote on my sheet.

Then, later, as a group we discussed budgets. I was afraid to tell everyone at my table that I had a hard time sticking to a budget. And in fact, I've always secretly felt that *God didn't love me because I couldn't stick to a budget.*

The workbook made it seem easy. All we had to do was write down everything we spend each day. Every day. For a month.

David and I looked at each other knowingly. We both knew that writing down everything seemed next to impossible. We are both right-brained, not really into structure and keeping track of things. We don't plan or schedule. We're free-spirited creative types, for better or for worse. It works well for us when we travel together, playing it by ear, letting our days unfold and being delighted in the outcome. Or when we pursue our creative passions of writing, playing music, or critiquing the latest exhibition at the Art Institute. But planning for the future, making a budget and sticking to it? Not so much.

So were we condemned to a life of poverty? Was something wrong with us? Would God still love us if we didn't write down what we spent every day for a month?

As the financial seminar wore on, I started picking up other messages from the leaders. The kind man at the podium started seeming a little less kind. In fact, he seemed to have been listening to Joel Osteen, the prosperity gospel guru. I heard things such as, "When you start tithing, you'll be surprised at how God provides for your needs!" or "When you stick to a budget, you'll be amazed at how money just appears in unexpected ways!"

There seemed to be some *quid pro quo* going on with God and money. If we stuck to a budget, got out of debt, and did everything right, then good things would happen, and God would bless us.

Sticking to a budget meant financial salvation. Not sticking to a budget meant we were lazy, undisciplined, and deserved the situation we were in.

Yet, I wasn't sure how David and I could work any harder. David was working three jobs. I was working full-time and freelancing on the side. We didn't have any more hours in the day to work. We were sticking to a budget as best as we could. Not perfectly, but given our personalities, I thought we were doing OK.

I also knew that when all was said and done, no matter how hard we worked, how closely we stuck to a budget, or how much I hung out with friends who are good at budgeting and paying off debt, that doesn't mean God would bring me wealth and happiness.

No amount of earning power or budgeting could guarantee financial salvation, or true abundance.

How did I come to equate material wealth with God's love?

I started noticing subtle messages all around me, such as those I'd heard at the financial seminar and from financial gurus. Riding the L to work, I saw an ad that said "America's Night of Hope" with Joel and Victoria. Apparently, these days Joel and Victoria Osteen didn't even need to include their last name on ads for their revival-style church meeting on August 6, 2011, at Cellular Field.

As I read the ad, I wondered, *What kind of hope?*

"God wants to give you your own house," Joel Osteen says in his book *Your Best Life Now.* "God wants us to prosper financially, to have plenty of money, to fulfill the destiny He has laid out for us."

Even though I've never set foot in a church that officially teaches the prosperity gospel, somehow it has seeped into my soul. It's come in through the back door and made itself cozy on my tattered couch. *If God wants to give me my own house, how come I still live in a small, two-bedroom condo? With a tattered couch?*

Prosperity theology or gospel (also known as the health-and-wealth gospel) proponents claim the Bible teaches that financial blessing is the will of God for Christians. And that Christians can achieve this through merely having faith, thinking positive thoughts, and maybe even donating to Christian ministries.

The prosperity gospel suggests that if God loves us, he doesn't want us to be poor.

In a *Time* poll, 17 percent of American Christians surveyed said they considered themselves part of such a movement, while a full 61 percent believed that God wants people to be prosperous. And 31 percent agreed that if you give your money to God, God will bless you with more money.

The prosperity gospel, combined with our entire capitalistic system, which is based on consumption, continually earning more money, and moving on up to bigger and better things, is a lethal combination.

The message in our culture constantly puts pressure on us to move onward and upward. If you don't, something is wrong with you.

I thought about these things as I stepped off the train when I went to work. I came face-to-face with people who didn't have a house. They didn't have a home at all. Apparently, they hadn't heard Joel and Victoria's message.

On my walk from the train station in downtown Chicago to my office on the north side of the "Loop," I walked about a mile. In that mile, I encountered five to ten homeless people along the sidewalk every day. *If these people are poor, does that mean God doesn't love them?*

The first person is usually standing outside the door of Ogilvie Station, holding a paper cup with a cardboard sign that reads: "Please help me pay for my medication." Occasionally there's a younger woman in the same area, with matted blonde hair and a dirt-caked coat who is obviously strung out on drugs, half out of it, holding a similar paper cup with a sign that tells passersby that she has a young son she's trying to support. I always wonder if "young son" really means "drug addiction."

Then, I walk a little further, and there is the man on the bridge that goes over the Chicago River. This guy, who dresses in layers and layers of warm clothes, even on a hot summer day, seems to suffer from a mental illness. His passionate monologue directed to passersby falls on deaf ears.

I cross the street to avoid an older, sad homeless man in a wheelchair selling *Street Wise*, the newspaper that the homeless in Chicago sell to make a little extra money. He sometimes wears a suit. He's scrubbed clean, and his skin stretches tight and shiny over his aging face, like a beach rock worn smooth from the tumbling and violence of the ocean waves.

I can't bear to see him, to imagine what his life is like. To wonder where he sleeps at night. To imagine how he ended up where he is.

But during the recession, the homeless in Chicago started looking different. I saw more women begging, more people who looked like—well, who looked like me.

When we were unemployed, there were times I felt that we were just a few financial steps away from being like the woman begging on the street corner or the man walking with a cardboard sign through the lines of cars stopped at an intersection.

If we couldn't come up with money for the mortgage. If we couldn't find freelance work. If we couldn't . . .

Now I could more easily relate to how a middle-class, employed, educated person could end up on the streets. How a financial house of cards could fall down completely with one small gust of misfortune.

Where before I felt compassion for the homeless and often tossed spare change into their paper cups, now I felt a kindred spirit. I didn't know what it was like to live on the streets, but all of a sudden I understood what financial desperation looked like. Of not being quite sure where the money would come from to pay for food. Of feeling that there were no options.

My deepening compassion was something I wanted. And it was something I wanted more than I wanted a new couch or a bigger house.

Monks know the virtues of living "close to the bottom." As Thomas Merton says in *New Seeds of Contemplation*, "The contemplative needs to be properly fed, clothed and housed. But he also needs to share something of the hardship of the poor. He needs to be able to identify himself honestly and sincerely with the poor, to be able to look at life through their eyes, and to do this because he is really one of them."

The Sermon on the Mount instructs us not to be anxious about material things, which is in direct contrast to our culture's message to buy more and more in order to be happy.

I started wondering if having more actually led us away from abundance. I read some research that seemed to suggest this was the case. Apparently, something happens when we acquire more and more stuff.

Berkeley psychologists Paul Piff and Dacher Keltner conducted studies to find out whether social class (having wealth, occupational prestige, and education) changes how we feel about others. The results of the studies suggest that wealth and status make us less compassionate and more self-focused. The participants of the study who had less income and education were more likely to feel compassion after watching a video about people suffering from cancer. Their heart rates slowed down, which is associated with paying greater attention to the feelings of others. The researchers' theory is that somehow wealth and abundance give us a sense of autonomy from others. The less we have to rely on other people, the less we may care about their feelings.[5]

Another study found that consumerism leads to depression. The study by Galen V. Bodenhausen and his colleague at Northwestern University suggests that people who place a high value on wealth, status, and material possessions may actually be the most depressed and antisocial among us.

Apparently Jesus was on to something when he said in Luke 12:32–33, "Do not be afraid, little flock, for it is your Father's good pleasure to give you the kingdom. Sell your possessions, and give alms" (New Revised Standard Version).

I thought it was curious that this verse would start with a command to not be afraid (something that is repeated over and over in Scripture). Then he calls us an endearing term, "little flock," and tells us it is our Father's good pleasure to give us the kingdom.

Then, finally, the verse ends with "Sell your possessions and give alms."

If material possessions and wealth lead us away from abundance, I wondered if financial poverty could actually be a key to experiencing the kingdom, of experiencing abundance. If I had many possessions to sell, I wondered if I would have the courage to do it for something as elusive as "the kingdom."

I found comfort in the fact that Jesus seemed to like to hang out with the poor, and that the people God uses the most are those who don't seem to have it all together. More and more, those are the kinds of people I wanted to hang out with too.

At a Christmas party, I talked to a friend who had been through two years of financial hell, similar to ours. A self-employed construction worker, his business had been slow due to the economy. He and his wife were raising four children and were trying to maintain the mortgage on a large house in the suburbs. They quickly realized they were in financial quicksand.

Paul would get a large job and earn some money, but they would get caught up on their mortgage payment only to find Paul having to go out and scramble for the next job. At the same time, their property taxes were skyrocketing. They were losing ground. Creditors were constantly calling them. They realized they would have to sell their house, probably for a loss, to get back on their feet. So they spent a year making repairs to their home, trying to get it ready to sell. It took another year before the house sold—for much less than they were hoping for. Now they are renting a small home.

"If we hadn't gone through the past two years," said Paul, "I wouldn't have grown closer to God. There were times that all I could do was call out to God. Before, I was just going through the motions with my faith."

He continued. "If I won the lottery tomorrow, sure it would be nice to not have to worry, but I think it takes a really special person to have a lot of money and still have a close relationship with God."

I was meeting weekly with a group from Old Saint Pat's to go through the spiritual exercises of St. Ignatius of Loyola. This Ignatian retreat was thirty-four weeks long, and about halfway through it, I discovered that St. Ignatius also struggled with this tug-of-war between wanting material wealth and yet wanting to be free from the desire for wealth. He was torn between the desire for wealth, which could ultimately lead to pride, and the way of Christ, which could lead to spiritual (and maybe material) poverty and humility and freedom. This wasn't just a problem I was confronting because I lived in 2011. Ignatius felt that struggle way back in the 1500s.

In his Spiritual Exercises, "The Fourth Day: A Meditation on Two Leaders, Two Strategies," (contemporary version) he writes, "People find themselves tempted to covet whatever seems to make them rich, and next because they possess some thing or things they find themselves pursuing and basking in the honor and esteem of this world. Then getting such deferences raises up the false sense of personal identity and value in which a blinding pride has its roots. . . . Lucifer's strategy is simple and seems so light-filled and clear in its direction: riches (or 'this is mine') to honor (or 'look at me') to pride (or 'I AM. . . .'). By these three steps, the evil one entices people to all other vices."[6]

And according to Ignatius, the way of Christ is a 180-degree turn in the opposite direction.

"Jesus adopts a strategy which directly opposes that of Lucifer: try to help and free people, not enslave or oppress them. . . . Jesus' strategy is simple too, although at first it seems a paradox. If I have been graced with the gift of poverty ('he emptied himself, becoming human'), then I am rich; if I have nothing of myself ('everything I have is from the Father'), I have no power and I am despised and receive the contempt of the world ('even to death, death on a cross'); if I have nothing, my only possession is Christ ('Christ is God's') and this is to be really true to myself—the humility of a person whose whole reality and value is grounded in being created and redeemed in Christ."[7]

In the traditional Spiritual Exercises, Ignatius instructed retreatants to pray for desiring the way of Christ at midnight, in the morning, and two other times during the day.

At our spiritual retreat weekly gathering, our leader led us through a meditation that helped us to imagine following these two opposite ways. We could desire the way of riches, which leads to power and recognition, which often leads to pride. Or we could imagine following the way of Christ—picturing Christ standing in an open field calling us to himself and his way. His way is the path of poverty of spirit (and maybe material poverty), which leads to lack of power, which in turn, leads to humility.

As I imagined these two options, I felt anxiety and ugliness when I thought of following the way of riches. That's what I'd been doing all this time—trying to attain material wealth and create my own "abundance" to help me feel like I was OK, that I was worth something, that I was secure and loved. That I mattered.

I was tired of it all. Plus, it wasn't working. Not only was I not able to attain material wealth, but also the striving for it left me depleted and empty. Plus, I didn't like where I thought it would lead me: to pride and self-satisfaction.

In contrast, thinking about the way of Christ felt freeing. What a relief it would be to stop caring about how much I had materially, or even how much I achieved or how I looked to others. To become more humble, and to live a life free from the striving. To rest in the peacefulness of knowing I am loved by God and that is enough.

I wanted to be like Dorothy Day, founder of the Catholic Worker movement, who chose a life of poverty. She said, "I'd like to live my life so close to the bottom that when the system collapses I don't have far to fall."

So I started praying the words of St. Ignatius:

Lord God, may
Nothing ever distract me from your love . . .
Neither health or sickness
Wealth or poverty
Honor nor dishonor
Long life or short life
May I never seek nor choose to be other
Than you wish or intend.
(italics mine)

As I prayed that prayer, the tug-of-war inside me ceased. Slowly, the desire for financial security, or material comforts, started losing its grip. I can't say exactly how it happened. But I told my spiritual director that I felt that I was on the right path. That maybe I had been on the right path all along and didn't even know it.

At Easter Vigil, I became a confirmed Catholic at Old Saint Pat's. I decided to take on the confirmation name "Saint Clare."

Clare of Assisi was one of the first followers of St. Francis of Assisi. She was the eldest daughter of Favorino Scifi, count of Sasso-Rosso, and his wife, Ortolana. Born to nobility, the beautiful young girl heard St. Francis preach and decided to follow him. Her family was livid. They wanted her to marry a young and wealthy man. But when she was eighteen, she heard Francis preach, and it changed her life.

Despite her family's objections, Clare left her castle home on the night of Palm Sunday of 1212 to commit her life to God. St. Francis cut off her beautiful golden hair, and she embraced a life of Gospel poverty, penance, and prayer.

She's often called "Poor Clare" because she came from a wealthy family and took a vow of poverty. The religious order she started became known as the Poor Clares.

"Behold, what I have desired, I now see; what I have hoped for, I now possess," wrote St. Clare after she left her worldly possessions behind and committed her life to God. "I am joined to him in heaven, whom I have loved on earth with my whole heart. I am espoused to him whom the angels serve, whose beauty the sun and moon admire."

On the night I was confirmed as a Catholic, my name tag was mistakenly missing my confirmation name. "Write it in," my sponsor, Karyn, whispered to me before the service.

"I don't know—is it that big of a deal?" I asked.

"Yes! You only get confirmed once."

So I borrowed her pen and wrote "Clare" between my first and last names, committing myself to leave behind my desire to strive for wealth. Later, the priest anointed me with oil by making a sign of the cross on my forehead and said, "Karen Clare Beattie. Be sealed with the gift of the Holy Spirit." I felt the warm oil on my forehead and prayed that it would be enough.

9
Baptized

My grandfather Wistrom, my mother's father, was a big Swedish man who played football in the early part of the twentieth century. He was around 6'3" and weighed around three hundred pounds. Here's what I remember about my grandfather. He could be loving. And he could be verbally abusive. He would give us a dime if we would tickle his arms as he napped on the floor, and he could berate our grandmother, yelling in anger at her and listing all of what he thought were her shortcomings, in our presence. He would whistle and sing as he lumbered around my grandparent's old farmhouse, and he could turn around and tell my anorexic sister how fat he thought she was. He would give us bear hugs but then shoot well-targeted criticism that would pierce the heart of his children and grandchildren.

This complicated, intimidating, damaged man had experienced a series of job setbacks that left him insecure and angry, and apparently he had deep wounds from his childhood. He took out his pain on my grandmother and my mother, aunt, and uncle.

My mom once told me that her father had told her over and over again: "You can't do anything right."

As a result, my mother tried to prove him wrong. She was driven, perfectionistic, and hard on herself and her own children. While she loved us well and the best she could—amazingly well, in fact, given the example of parenting she'd had—the damage trickled down to us.

My mother wanted me, and all of her daughters, to be an accomplished pianist in the worst way. She played the piano and wanted us to take piano lessons while we were young. I practiced and tried to live up to her expectations. But if a passion isn't also inside a child's heart, it's difficult to make that child live out a parent's dream that isn't also her dream and try to force her to make up for the parent's inadequacies.

Once, when I was very young, around seven, my mom volunteered me to play a solo in a New Year's Eve service at the Adelphi Calvary Baptist church. She didn't ask me. She just told me I was going to do it. The only song I had rehearsed was "Silent Night," and since Christmas was over, I was embarrassed to be playing a Christmas song on New Year's Eve. Wouldn't it be odd? It was the wrong holiday! Nevertheless, I practiced and practiced, my stomach in knots at the thought of playing a solo in front of a hundred or so people.

The night of the solo, I wore my best holiday dress. It was scratchy and stiff. When it was time for my solo, I walked up the green-sculpted-carpet aisle and up the four steps to the stage, to the grand piano. With some embarrassment, I put the sheet music for my Christmas song on the ledge of the piano. I put my shaking fingers on the cool, ivory keys, and all of a sudden I forgot everything that I had been rehearsing. The notes were a blur.

I pressed my fingers down on the keys and tried to start playing. In fits and starts I made it through the first few measures, but it was a jumble of notes. As I made my way through the song, I could feel the eyes of the congregants staring at me. My stomach churned. My face burned bright red. Tears were forming in my throat and making their way up to my eyes.

I finally got to the end, and because of misplaced fingers, ended the song on a dissonant chord, putting a fitting ending to a miserable solo.

The church was silent except for the echo of the dissonant chord bouncing off the ceiling and walls.

No one at my church ever clapped; that would be irreverent inside the church. But they typically said hearty *amens!* after an especially great number during the service. After my solo, I heard a few weak amens scattered around the congregation, but I could tell they were spoken mostly to be polite.

I grabbed my sheet music, left the piano quickly, and slunk back to the pew with my head down and my face burning, wanting to cry. On my way to sit down, I glanced up at my mom, hoping for some reassurance.

Instead, her eyes were slits, her head tilted, her lips pursed. I knew that look. It said: "How could you embarrass me like that? Shame!"

I sat in the pew and stared at the floor.

I was a quiet, introverted child who tended to sit around and daydream, draw, and write poetry. My mother was always prodding me to "do something!" "Be productive!" making me feel that my personality was somehow flawed, that what I brought to the table wasn't enough. That I needed to be more outgoing, more assertive, more driven, more action oriented.

I felt that I could never do enough, or accomplish enough, or look good enough to win Mom's love. She felt imperfect, so she tried to force perfection in everything around her, including her children, as a poor compensation.

While I tried my best to live up to her expectations throughout my childhood, it seemed that I was always falling short. Mom tried to teach me to sew, but she would end up ripping out the crooked seams I sewed and making me do it over and over until I got it right.

In high school, on the eve of our team's regional tournament debut, she sat down on my bed and told me she really wanted our team to win the state tournament—because when she played basketball in high school, she always regretted that her team didn't win. But now I had a chance to help my team get to state, if I played hard enough. When our team was eliminated from the tournament a few games later, I felt like a failure.

Even though deep down I knew Mom loved me, the mixed messages she sent left me doubting who I was and whether or not I deserved to be loved. While she never said the same words, the message "You can never do anything right!" from her father had trickled down a generation to me.

Later in life, when I was in my thirties, my mother seemed to know that she had wounded me and tried to reverse the damage. Once, when she was visiting me in Chicago, I was getting ready to go out to a friend's birthday party. It was a dress-up affair, and I was putting on a black tank top and dressy black pants. I invited my parents to come along, but Mom and Dad were going to stay at my apartment and relax after a busy day of sightseeing and shopping.

As we were talking and I finished putting on my red lipstick, she looked at me and said, "I just think you're the neatest girl. I'm so proud of you." I just looked at her and smiled, but her words started to heal the little cracks in my soul.

I had chosen a different life from hers. She hadn't gone to college; I had earned a Master's degree. She had stayed in a small town in Iowa; I had moved to the big city. I had a career; she had been a stay-at-home mom most of her adult life. I think I always wondered if she was disappointed that I hadn't found a nice, rich, Christian man to settle down with. But I think there was a part of her that admired my independence, my life in the city, my freedom.

One of the last times I saw her was a few years later, in the fall of 2000, before I'd met and married David. She and Dad had come to visit me in Chicago. It was September, and it was hot—unusually hot. It was miserable taking them around to all the tourist destinations. But we took an architectural tour on the Chicago River, went to the Chicago Botanic Garden, and heard an outdoor concert at Ravinia. Throughout the weekend, my mom kept buying me things. She had always liked to buy me things, but this was excessive. A new watch. Things for my apartment. Clothes. While I never felt that she understood me when I was a child, her carefully selected gifts always seemed to be spot-on. Although she couldn't connect emotionally, she totally got me when it came to her gifts. "Mom, you don't have to do this," I told her that weekend. But she insisted.

On Sunday, after church, they left to drive the six hours home to Iowa. I hugged both of them in the entryway of my apartment. My mom had tears in her eyes when she looked at me from the doorway.

I watched out my front windows as their car drove away.

Three months later, I drove home to Iowa from Chicago the day before Christmas Eve. This was long before I met David and gotten married. I was used to driving to Iowa alone, but this time I asked a friend from church, Loren, to drive with me because it had been a horribly snowy, cold December, and I was afraid of driving on the icy highways by myself. I had also asked Loren to ride with me because I had been experiencing an odd sort of restlessness that autumn and December. I couldn't put my finger on it, but I had been suffering from a deep sadness mixed with anticipation—a feeling that something was shifting, that I was waiting for something to happen but I didn't know what.

I was freelancing at the time, and I could barely sit down to work. The prospect of driving home to Iowa on a snowy Interstate 80 was more than I could bear, so I asked Loren to go with me.

I picked up Loren at his condo around ten in the morning, and we started driving west, out of the city on the Eisenhower Expressway, then on I-88 into rural Illinois. We had to drive slowly because the roads were bad and it was snowing, so we didn't get to Iowa City (where Loren's parents lived) until 4:30 or so, and it was already dark outside. I went into his home to greet his parents and then left to finish the hour-and-a-half drive home.

Before I got back onto I-80, I stopped at a gas station to fill the tank. I hadn't looked at my cell phone all day, because back then, twelve years ago, we didn't use them constantly. I took my phone with me on trips as a safety precaution, in case I had a flat tire or got lost. But I took out my cell phone to call home, to let them know I'd be arriving a little later than usual because of the weather.

My brother answered the phone at my parent's house. It didn't seem unusual that he would be there.

"Where are you?" he asked.

I thought it was an odd question, or maybe I sensed something odd in his tone. "I'm in Iowa City. I should be home in a few hours."

There was silence. Then I could hear him turn to others in the room and say, "She's in Iowa City."

I knew something was wrong. I could tell in his voice. "Why? What's wrong?" I asked.

"Just come home," he said.

"No—tell me what's wrong." I could feel panic moving up my chest into my throat. My first thought was that something had happened to my sister and her family, who were driving from Ohio. Maybe they had gotten in an accident. "Just tell me, Scott. What's wrong?"

Finally, he said, "Mom died this morning."

The snow was collecting at the base of the gas pump. It was dark, but the florescent lights of the gas station cast an eerie light onto the front seat of the car.

I couldn't absorb this news. I put my head on the steering wheel as my brother continued to talk. She had died at around eleven, as she was wrapping gifts for her children and grandchildren. It was a heart attack or a stroke. Whatever it was, it took her quickly, and there was nothing the paramedics—who had taken ages to get there because of the snow—could do. She was only sixty-three.

We discussed logistics. I couldn't drive the rest of the way home. It was cold, snowing, and dark, and my mother had just died. I was in no condition to drive.

I went back to Loren's parents' house, and when he greeted me at the door, I collapsed into my friend's arms. The rest of the evening is a blur. I called my brother again from their phone; Scott offered to drive part of the way to Iowa City to pick me up. Loren would drive my car, and we would meet Scott in Grinnell, which was halfway between Iowa City and Des Moines.

As Loren drove us west, I couldn't get my head around the fact that my mother was gone. She would never see me get married, or meet my children. I would never have the chance to become better friends with her. In a fundamental part of me, the world had ended.

Scott picked me up, and we drove the rest of the way to Des Moines. As we drove into the driveway, my aunt and uncle were driving in, too. I got out of the car, and their arms wrapped around me, and we stood there for a few minutes, huddled together in a group hug in the frigid December air.

The next morning, the sun rose, and I was shocked that the world kept going on as if nothing had happened. My father and I sat at the kitchen table, after a night of not really sleeping, and we looked out at the deck, where a sparrow lay dead and frozen—after flying into the windows. Another sparrow was standing over it, as if it were keeping watch for its dead friend. Or maybe they were partners. Or the dead bird was its mother.

I thought of my mom's wispy gray hair, her pretty smile, her hands that had become rough from years of scrubbing and cleaning, as she tried to create a perfectly clean house. I thought of her excitement about Christmas, and her obsession to make it perfect for all of us. She was passionate about a holiday for which she could buy just the right gift for everyone.

On Christmas morning, we were left looking at the gifts she was wrapping when she died. Her final gifts to us.

What should we do? Open them? Leave them wrapped? In the end, two days after my mother died, we moved ahead with Christmas morning. We adults would have preferred to skip any type of tradition, but the grandchildren, who couldn't yet comprehend the finality of the death of their grandmother, were still expecting gifts.

Terry Nelson-Johnson says, "The ultimate abundance is knowing oneself as loved, and it's not currency, it's available . . . and it's ridiculous in its lavishness, regardless of my circumstances."

I had been equating God's love with the wrong things—feeling loved only when my circumstances were going my way, my bank account was full, my dreams were on track, and I was a success.

The key is to remember that we *are* baptized—not *were* baptized. Matthew 3:16–17 says:

> When Jesus had been baptized, just as he came up from the water, the heavens were opened to him, and he saw the Spirit of God descending like a dove and alighting on him. And a voice from heaven, said, "This is my Son, the Beloved, with whom I am well pleased."
>
> —New Revised Standard Version

I thought back on my baptism. I was baptized at Adelphi Calvary Baptist church, the same church where I experienced my piano solo shame.

The baptismal tank had a cheesy mountain lake scene wallpapered above it. We were in the middle of Iowa. I could never figure out why we had a mountain scene above the baptismal tank. Maybe we were aspiring to greater things. When the curtains opened, I stepped down the steps and let the hem of my white gown float up in the tepid water. I stood with the pastor, and when he asked if I believed in Christ as my savior and had asked "Jesus into my heart," I said yes. Then I put my hands up to my face and plugged my nose as he tipped me back and dunked my whole body.

I rose up out of the water and, barely tall enough to see over the tank, looked out at the congregation who had witnessed my profession of faith. Aunts and uncles, neighbors, my sisters and brother and cousins. My parents. I felt good to be pleasing my parents and aunts and uncles. But at the time, I didn't really understand the depth of what I was doing.

Early Christians were baptized in a river. The person being baptized would walk into the river wearing an old, rough gown. The moving river would "wash away" sin—or whatever was keeping her from experiencing full communion with God—and once on the other side, she would take off the rough, old garment and put on a bright white new one. New life.

Terry says that once you know you are baptized, you're free. The particular grace of baptism is to know, viscerally know, that you are radically, passionately, irrevocably, ridiculously, tenaciously, and desperately loved by the Author of love.

I couldn't hear that truth back then when I was baptized. I was only seven, and the baptismal tank was only ten feet away from the piano where I had experienced my New Year's Eve shame.

I couldn't hear the truth about God's love for many years. I did not have the ears to hear. Nor did my mother, I realize now. There were too many other voices—voices of shame, and worthlessness, and perfectionism. These voices were telling me that I didn't deserve to become a mother. That I didn't deserve to have abundance. That I was not worthy. That I should be ashamed. And I saw a face with a pursed mouth and squinted eyes looking at me as if to say, "How could you embarrass me like that?"

I couldn't hear the truth for many years, but slowly, to the sounds of clanking L trains above my head on my walk to work, in the midst of the busses belching diesel fumes as they sped by on the city streets, in the middle of the crowded, frantic, concrete city, I heard the warblers singing and the wind gently blowing through the blooms on the Downy Hawthorn trees along the Chicago River.

Slowly, I heard it, and it started sinking into my soul. This voice that I had longed to hear all my life was calling to me, and I finally heard what it was telling me:

You.

Are.

My.

Beloved.

Daughter.

In.

Whom.

I.

Am.

Well.

Pleased.

10

The Dance

The trouble is
that I'd let my gestures freeze.
The trouble was not
in the kitchen or the tulips
but only in my head, my head.

Then all this became history.
Your hand found mine.
Life rushed to my fingers like a blood clot.
Oh, my carpenter,
the fingers are rebuilt.
They dance with yours.
They dance in the attic and in Vienna.
My hand is alive all over America.
Not even death will stop it,
death shedding her blood.
Nothing will stop it, for this is the kingdom
and the kingdom come.

—from "The Touch," by Anne Sexton

In the spring of 2011, I finally got to go to a prom.

To raise money for the Beloved Retreats, the Beloved community decided to hold a dance. Not just any dance. This would be known as "The Beloved Prom."

Decades after I hid in the back of my dad's Cadillac, looking into the gym at the other high schoolers dancing at the prom, I was going to go to the Beloved Prom decked out in a black cocktail dress. David, my date, had on a black suit with a gray shirt and black tie. He looked hot. I was hoping we'd make out in the car after the dance.

We arrived at Old Saint Pat's; the Prom was in the "church hall" (aka: the basement). There were streamers. There was a disco ball. There were prom dresses—huge taffeta numbers that friends had found in secondhand stores.

"Come even if you look like Elaine Benes on *Seinfeld* when you dance!" Terry had announced weeks earlier.

His invitation to all of us bad dancers made me feel a little better. You see, when you grow up in a strict fundamentalist home, you don't really learn how to dance. While all those other kids were learning how to square dance in Runnells Elementary School gym class, a few other Baptist kids and I were sitting on the sidelines. We were conscientious objectors. And while my high school friends were perfecting their dance moves at homecoming dances and proms all across America in the early 1980s, I was at home watching *Starsky and Hutch*.

Now, thirty years later, I still felt that I hadn't caught up on learning my dance moves. I tended to move around the dance floor tentatively, like an old lady with arthritis.

But by this time, I was pretty much doing anything Terry suggested, so despite my trepidation, I brought my Baptist butt to the Beloved Prom.

Terry, in his Birkenstocks, served as the MC. "An early name for God is 'The Dance,'" Terry told us. "Not even 'He Dances,' but 'The Dance.'"

So he told us to go out there on the dance floor and imitate God, The Dance. Even if we looked silly.

The music began, and Father Paul started us off with a solo dance number. His awkward dancing made us all feel a little less self-conscious about or own dancing abilities.

Then, Bob and Jill, who had told their story of sorrow and had danced at the very first Beloved Retreat I had attended shortly after my layoff, started dancing. They looked beautiful dancing together, Jill wearing her deceased daughter's dancing shoes. They made us all feel a little intimidated because they seemed to float across the floor. They didn't look like Elaine Benes at all.

Kate and Pete, who had become good friends, were at the dance, and so were Alexis and Eugene, a couple our age who also didn't have children. Then I ran into Laura, my spiritual director, whom I hugged.

After sitting on the sidelines at the table for a while, I was starting to feel like the left-out child again. I had to do it, just go out there on the dance floor and not care how I looked.

I mustered up the courage to dance. I pulled David out of his chair and onto the floor. We laughed at how silly we looked. But we were surrounded by people who loved us and didn't care.

Later, a couple who ran a dance studio taught the whole group how to rumba. They looked as if they were straight out of *Dancing with the Stars*—gaudy, sequined costumes and all.

David and I moved our feet to the music, dancing together and laughing. We had been through so much in the past few years—two miscarriages, job struggles, grief. But I felt so free now, moving my feet, swaying to the music.

I danced with Jack, a friend who had just been diagnosed with Parkinson's disease and was going through a divorce. I danced with Alexis and Eugene and Pete and Kate in one big circle. I danced with new friends who were teaching me how to see God in a new way. I just danced.

We all looked awkward (except Bob and Jill). But this was my community. We were all broken but whole. I looked around and drank in the beautiful, imperfect, wonderful richness.

11

How the Paschal Mystery Saved My Faith

Time does goes on—
I tell it gay to those who suffer now—
They shall survive—
There is a sun—
They don't believe it now—

—Emily Dickinson

I was twelve when a fistfight broke out on the front lawn of the Adelphi Calvary Baptist Church, the church my ancestors founded. It happened after a particularly contentious business meeting one warm Sunday evening, as groups of congregants stood on the front porch talking. We looked on in horror as two of the deacons started yelling and then lunged at each other.

They were fighting over a disagreement that had started in the business meeting—over the color of the new carpet, or whether the church covenant should be displayed in the sanctuary, or the type of grape juice we should use for communion. I can't remember the trivial subject that launched the fight. But we stood around them watching, and drivers on the highway in front of the church slowed down to see what was happening.

We were all mortified. It wasn't exactly the "testimony" that we, as a church, were aiming to present to our secular neighbors who were driving by.

We stood and watched as the deacons punched each other in the face, and two other deacons grabbed them and pulled them apart.

But before the ruckus was over, my parents herded all of us kids and put us in the big Cadillac.

After years of enduring the bickering and infighting in that small church, my parents had had enough. We drove out of the driveway of the Adelphi Calvary Baptist Church, never to return.

That was the church where I had spent many hours sitting on the pews, my gangly legs sticking to the gooey varnish. It was the church that I could see from my bedroom window, where most of our family and friends attended. I was baptized there, and there I learned all those old hymns that I can still hear in my head. In that church we had eaten potluck dinners of hamburger casseroles, Jell-O, and green-bean salads. We had played on the big hilly front lawn with our friends after Sunday school, and we'd spent early Easter morning sunrise services there, with pancake breakfasts afterwards. In that church, I had "asked Jesus into my heart" (many times, just to be sure. I was a little obsessive-compulsive).

I remember standing in the front of that sanctuary, after my baptism, and my great aunt, with her grey-blue hair came up to me. She told me that if my grandmother, who had died five months before I was born, had been there, she would have been so proud.

I had watched my mother play the organ in that sanctuary every Sunday morning. The people in that community were the friends we spent summers with at the Iowa Regular Baptist Camp. My aunt Colleen had taught me Bible stories in Sunday school, carefully placing the Bible characters on the flannel background as she told the stories. This was the church that formed my early faith—for better or for worse.

Leaving that church was like leaving our whole lives behind.

After that, we drove all the way into the city and across town to the Airport Baptist Church (creative name—it was by the airport). This church was a bit bigger (it was in the city! Des Moines!) and had a bigger youth group. My older sisters already knew some of the kids in that church because they had met them at camp the summer before. But I didn't know anyone.

The first Sunday we arrived, my older sister introduced me to the younger sister, Lori, of her friend Trina. Lori was a year younger than me, but I was drawn to her dark curly hair and her confidence. She was in charge, a "city girl."

Lori led me to the part of the church where the Sunday school rooms were. We walked into a pink room with pink shag carpeting. It was the sixth-grade Sunday school room. There I met Sheri Jutting, Lori's friend, who would turn out to be a lifelong friend. After that, the three of us were inseparable; enjoying sleepovers and hanging out together at youth group events and during Sunday school.

I stayed at that church all through high school and college. There are good memories of youth group outings, mission trips, and Mike, our hilarious youth group leader. Those experiences formed my faith in critical ways. But later I found out (after I had moved to Chicago) that there had been financial indiscretion within the church leadership, there was fallout, and after that, the church community never really fully recovered.

In my twenties I attended a nondenominational evangelical church that seemed hip and cool at the time; we met in the dark theater of an expensive private high school in Lincoln Park in Chicago. The church was filled with twenty- and thirty-something singles. But underneath the veneer of the cool, urban, seemingly progressive church was a theology that looked curiously like the fundamentalism I had grown up with. Forty-minute sermons seemed designed to pound our heads with the message. There was an attempt to explain and interpret everything, to deliver answers that seemed too certain and tied up neatly in a bow.

The men (always men) in the pulpit had good intentions. But the constant attempts to understand and have everything nailed down caused my faith to wither.

Eventually I left that church when there was a huge rift after the pastor was asked to leave because of some vague infidelity.

I have watched three churches fall apart. I have experienced the disappointment in leadership, the disillusionment of congregants who put all their faith into the leadership. I became exhausted by the focus on things that didn't seem to matter.

And that old fundamentalist faith I had grown up with didn't fit anymore. As if it were a too-small winter coat, I shrugged it off and was out in the cold without a church community to keep me warm for two or three years.

Sunday mornings turned into peaceful times at the coffee shop reading the *New York Times* and sipping a latte. Church? I didn't miss it that much.

If I was going to continue the Christian journey, I wanted it to be authentic. A faith that fit. A faith that drew me higher up and deeper in. A faith motivated by love, not by judging people on whether or not they were doing everything right. A place that could hold all my questions.

For a time I joined a tiny congregation that was trying to do church in a new way. Dave, our "pastor," talked about narrative theology. How we are part of the story of God working in his people's lives.

Narrative theology, I learned, was inspired by a group of theologians such as George Lindbeck, Hans Wilhelm Frei, and others at the Yale Divinity School. They were influenced by Karl Barth, Thomas Aquinas, and to some extent, the *nouvelle théologie*, a school of thought proposing reform in the Catholic Church, led by French Catholics such as Henri de Lubac.

Narrative theology is the idea that Christian theology's use of the Bible should focus on a narrative representation of the faith rather than the development of a set of propositions reasoned from the Scriptures themselves or what is commonly called a "systematic theology." Basically, narrative theology is a fairly broad term, but oftentimes it is that approach to theology that primarily looks to the meaning in story. At other times, narrative theology is associated with the idea that we are not primarily to learn principles, rules or laws from Scripture, but rather we are to learn to relate to God, and how to play our part in the greater panorama of our salvation. Narrative theology teaches that the Bible is seen as the story of God's interaction with His people.[8]

I liked that, because it was about a story. And a vision. Not just about dos and don'ts and a set of propositions to be proven in a forty-five-minute sermon.

"We can choose which story we want to follow," I remember Dave saying. "I choose to follow the story of Christ."

The Bible, then, became a collection of stories—still divinely inspired but interacting in the lives of God's people. A story that showed God's love and power in Christ's life, death, and resurrection. It was a story of transformation and Christ's kingdom.

But the small storefront church and community that my pastor friend had started was struggling. We were a small community, and people started going their own ways. Dave eventually ended up as the pastor of a small church in the northwestern suburbs of Chicago.

When I met the man I was going to marry, I had been spending my Sundays again in the coffee shop reading. I read authors such as Henri Nouwen, Thomas Merton, and Kathleen Norris. I was drawn to Catholic theologians, or at least to authors who had that type of leaning. And to the mystics.

While I was drawn to certain Catholic writers, whom I heard referred to as the prophets of the Catholic Church (as opposed to "the management"), I stayed away from the Catholic Church because it seemed too austere, scary, and hierarchical. Plus, my Baptist mother would have turned over in her grave if she knew I was going to a Catholic church. And all those scandals? Who would want to join a church like that?

But when you fall in love, all rational thought goes out the window. At least that's what happened when I fell in love with my husband. And it's what happened when I fell in love with a church.

When I met David in 2004, I was taken over by some uncontrollable force that made me a little crazy for a while. Then, eight months later, I was married to this guy I barely knew (yet felt that I'd known all my life) and wondered what in the heck had just happened.

The same thing happened to me when I set foot inside a Catholic congregation in downtown Chicago. Soon after we were married, David and I searched for a church community together, visiting many churches of various denominations. One sunny summer morning, we stepped into Old Saint Pat's sanctuary, and we felt as if we were inside a giant, magnificent Easter egg. More important, we felt as if we were home.

I could sense the Holy Spirit there. The place was alive and buzzing. People paid attention to the homilies. Everyone was friendly and warm. I had never been to a church where the passing of the peace was carried out with so much enthusiasm and vigor. Plus, this new expression of my faith was dressed in stained-glass windows, marble floors, soaring ceilings, and new language.

How could this be? After all, many people had been *leaving* the Catholic Church, for what I thought were understandable reasons. Why was I feeling so drawn to it?

But David and I kept going to Mass, and rituals and traditions that seemed mysterious and strange at first came to have meaning.

I learned that the sign of the cross had been a signal by which persecuted Christians during the first century used to discretely greet other Christians on the streets of Rome. With this signal, they affirmed their belief in the divinity and humanity of Christ.

I learned that Catholics dipped their fingers into the font at the back of the sanctuary and made the sign of the cross to remind themselves of their baptisms. The rituals, liturgy, and homilies added a new dimension to my faith, a deeper understanding of what it means to follow Christ.

A few years after we started attending that church, I decided to make a commitment. But first, I had to make sure, despite my irrational feelings, that I was making the right decision.

I grilled the poor RCIA leaders: What about infant baptism? Do Catholics believe that only Catholics are going to heaven? What is heaven, anyway? And what is sin? How can I become Catholic if I don't believe everything the pope says? Do the bread and the wine *literally* become the body of Christ? And would Catholics discount the faith I had lived during the past forty years? For me, becoming Catholic wasn't a conversion as much as an evolution of the faith I had been living most of my life.

My RCIA leaders told me later that, more than once, they thought I was going to bolt. They may have been right; I kept waiting for the deal breaker.

It never came. The leaders listened to my questions compassionately, thoughtfully—and patiently. Most important, they gave me permission to ask questions and were humble enough to admit that they didn't have all the answers.

In the end, all the questions I had, and all the answers that were given, didn't really matter. I was going to become part of this church, for better or for worse, because the Holy Spirit was calling me here and I couldn't resist. And this faith tradition was big enough to hold all my questions.

It was at this church where I first heard the term *paschal mystery.* But I had experienced it years before.

In the months that followed my mother's death, I realized that she had left us all one last gift. Strange things happened that never would have happened if this tragedy had not struck our family.

Losing my mother brought the rest of us closer together. Old resentments melted away. Things I had never been able to say to my father just spilled from me, and I was able to tell him how much I loved him. I became closer to my sisters and brother. Extended family members gathered around us, like a protective wall against the grief. Stoic northern Europeans, we now expressed freely how much we loved one another.

But the grief itself was the most interesting thing. It changed me. It changed my relationships. I became more compassionate and more honest. More authentic.

What was happening? How could I actually be grateful that my mother had died? It seemed inconceivable. Was I dishonoring her? Or could these two things coexist: the grief and loss, along with the gratefulness?

But as I learned more about the paschal mystery, I started understanding that the Christian life is about sharing in Christ's life, death, and resurrection and letting it transform you. I read somewhere that the key to understanding the Paschal Mystery is the Hebrew word *pesah* or *pesach,* which means to pass over, to skip. To go across.

Passover is a Jewish festival that commemorates the story of the Exodus, in which the Israelites were freed from slavery. In the well-known biblical story, the Israelites were instructed to mark the doorposts of their homes with the blood of a lamb, and thus the spirit of the Lord would see the blood and pass over the firstborn in these homes, sparing them from death (Exodus 12:13).

It's interesting that the Israelites were spared from the curse of the tenth and worst plague by killing a lamb. But it's also interesting to note the symbolism of the story: Crossing over from slavery to freedom is possible only through the death of the lamb. Freedom involves death. How can we cross over to new life, then, without having to pass through suffering?

I was beginning to realize that there is no resurrection without dying. There is no Easter without Good Friday. There is no joy without grief. There is no spring without winter. I felt as if I'd spent so much time in the Holy Thursdays and Good Fridays of life. But those are the times when I had grown the most.

Throughout my childhood, I had been seeing my faith through the lens of atonement theology—a theology that says Jesus died for our sins, therefore we are saved. That kind of theology places us on the sidelines, thanking Christ for his sacrifice.

But the paschal mystery invites us to join Christ in his suffering. Holy Thursday, Good Friday, Holy Saturday, and Easter—all are full of grace.

One day I was talking with my friend Mary on the phone about the verse "I came that you might have life, and have it more abundantly."

"You know," Mary said, "people misread that verse all the time. That verse doesn't say, 'I came that you might have abundance.' It really says, 'I came that you might have life'—life in all its joys and sorrows and ups and downs, life in all its chaos."

All these years, my mind had just kind of skipped over the word *life* and gone right to the idea of abundance.

As I contemplated what the verse really means, I realized that experiencing abundant life has more to do with living fully, of being awake and not afraid to experience fully all the ups and downs, the good times and the hard times.

I remembered the months after my mother died, when my whole family, but especially my dad, was stuck in the Good Friday of loss. Every time I talked to him on the phone, words would get caught in his throat as he tried to stem the flow of tears. For two years, I heard those tears in my dad's voice.

But he forced himself to get out of the house. Even when he didn't want to, he went to church. He visited my aunt and uncle. He went to work. "I'm not going to sit around and feel sorry for myself," he told me.

I hated the thought of him cooking dinner for himself or learning how to use the washer and dryer.

A few months after Mom died, I drove to Iowa to visit Dad. I felt a knot in my stomach when I walked into the house and my mom wasn't there to greet me. I made the bed in the guest room and cleaned out the refrigerator, which was filled with milk containers months past their expiration date and half-eaten takeout meals.

Late one night, Dad knocked on the guest bedroom door. It must have been about midnight. I was startled, and my thoughts immediately went to everything that could be wrong. Was he having a heart attack? Was there some sort of emergency?

But instead, he said in a loud whisper, "Karen, come here, I have to show you something."

I threw on my robe and followed him to his bedroom window. I looked out, and there in the moonlight, I could see a herd of deer curled up underneath the big oak tree in our front yard, asleep and huddled together to ward off the cold. The bright moonlight reflected off the snow and their smooth, silky winter coats. Tiny fawns, the size of stuffed animals, were curled up next to their mothers. As we looked at the sleeping mass of fur, a doe raised her head and looked toward us, sensing that someone was watching her.

"Isn't that something?" my father said softly. Instead of tears, his voice was filled with awe and wonder.

As David and I were recovering from the darkest moments of our financial crisis and the death of our dreams, I was beginning to see the good that could come from the pain. The community at Old Saint Pat's, and the stories I heard there, helped me believe there was hope for resurrection. I could relate to St. Augustine, who wrote, "In my deepest wound I saw Your glory and it dazzled me."

12
The Whirlwind

I wanted a perfect ending. Now I've learned, the hard way, that some poems don't rhyme, and some stories don't have a clear beginning, middle, and end. Life is about not knowing, having to change, taking the moment and making the best of it, without knowing what's going to happen next.

—Gilda Radner

During the summer when I was growing up in Iowa, we'd look at the sky at dusk. After a day of playing hard outside, we'd join my dad, who loved to sit on the porch and watch the sunset.

Maybe it was because my father grew up in a farming family and the weather determined whether it would be a good or bad year, and when they could put the crops in, or begin harvesting the corn and soybeans. But weather was woven into the fabric of our lives, and our eyes were always turned upward.

During the summer, we were on the lookout for storms. Living in a big, drafty farmhouse, with windows that rattled in the wind, didn't help a child who was frightened of storms. And that big old farmhouse sat high up on a hill, a perfect target for lightning, I thought, as I huddled in the bottom bunk in my bedroom on the top floor of the house.

My father, tucking us into bed at night, assured us that the lightning was far, far away. "See," he said, "You just have to count and see how long it takes to hear the thunder."

If the lightning was close, the light and sound would happen simultaneously. But if it took a few seconds from the time the lightning flashed in the sky until the *boom!* of the thunder, we knew that we weren't in danger.

I huddled in the bottom bunk, and counted "onethousandone, onethousandtwo, onethousand three . . ." *Boom!*

If the storm was really bad, my father listened on the radio for any tornado warnings. If it was during the day, we could see the wall of clouds coming from the horizon. In Iowa, on the hill where our house sat, we could see for miles and miles across the Des Moines River valley. We could tell if a storm was brewing; we would watch the clouds churning with black, blue, gray, and pink, with sparks of lightning flashing in short bursts, showing the outlines of the high, cumulus clouds.

But at night, we could trust only the weather forecasters and hope they could warn us in time if a tornado was on the way.

Many times my dad would walk down the hall to my room, which I shared with my sister Sara, and the room across the hall, where my older two sisters slept. Scott slept in the room next to my parents' room.

If we were half asleep, my parents would carry us down to the basement, where we would huddle against the cold, cinder-block wall, and listen to the radio, the wind punching the basement windows so hard we thought they would break.

Only once did a tornado hit our little corner of the world. We were at a swimming meet in Indianola, which was twenty miles or so south of where we lived. During the swimming meet, we noticed the beautiful clouds forming in the sky—interesting shades of green, yellow, and pink. We didn't realize that those clouds were churning into a massive thunderstorm.

On our drive home, we saw the lightning to the north. Then, as we drove into the storm, the rain was like metal pellets against the windshield. It was evening and getting dark. Our cousins lived on the route home, so we stopped there to take shelter, staying until the storm passed. Then we drove, slowly, the last five miles home.

We could see the damage as we drove down Vandalia Drive, our street. The steeple of the Adelphi Calvary Baptist church was gone. So was the garage of the parsonage, toppled like a tower of Legos at the hands of a toddler.

Then we drove by my grandfather's house. The huge old barn behind his house had been lifted up by the winds and then set down right next to the foundation.

As we drove up our driveway, we could see our garage listing severely to the right. It looked as if it would topple over at any minute.

Dad went into the house first, to see if it was safe for us to go in. When we went inside, we found the floor of the kitchen covered in an inch of water because we had left some of the windows open. But otherwise, our house was intact.

Those beautiful clouds we saw at the swimming meet had sent a tornado crashing uncontrollably into our little part of the world, and for a time our lives were turned upside down. The next day we surveyed the damage and talked to neighbors, all of us agreeing that we were fortunate no one had been injured or killed.

There's a tornado in the last scene of *A Serious Man*. For the longest time, I couldn't figure out why. At this point in the movie, things are looking up for Larry Gopnik. His son has made it through his bar mitzvah; his colleague tells him he will probably get tenure after all; and his wife's lover dies in a car crash, paving the way for Larry to reconcile with her. Things are still a bit tenuous, but there is a little of light on the horizon.

But then Larry decides to change the grade of the student who has been bribing and blackmailing him. He erases the F and changes it

to a C. He needs the bribe money to help his brother, who has gotten into trouble with the law.

As soon as Larry changes the grade, his phone rings. It is his doctor. We are left with the impression that Larry's doctor has some bad
news. Is this a direct result of his "sin"? We don't know but are left to
wonder.

In the very last scene of the film, Larry's son is at school, and all
the children are ordered to seek shelter because there is a storm coming. The children go outside to find shelter at a nearby building. The
closing scene is of the school children, including Larry's son, turning
around and seeing a raging tornado coming toward them.

The end.

It was months after I saw the film (and actually had watched it
again) that I was reading a book about Job and decided to look at
the original Scripture.

Then, there it was. The ending of the Coen brothers' film.

In the book of Job, the first thirty-seven chapters consist of Job's
complaints against God. After having lost everything, he has a lot to
rant about. But a curious thing happens in chapter 38. God finally
speaks. And he does it in a whirlwind—a tornado.

> Then the LORD answered Job out of the whirlwind, and said, "Who
> is this that darkeneth counsel by words without knowledge? Gird up
> now thy loins like a man; for I will demand of thee, and answer
> thou me. Where wast thou when I laid the foundations of the earth?
> declare, if thou hast understanding."
>
> —Job 38:1–4, King James Version

Job is speechless. After thirty-seven chapters of questioning and
lament and anger at God, he finally stands face-to-face with the
awesomeness of the Divine and has nothing to say. He questions
melt away.

The summer of 2011 brought many storms to Chicago. Every other week, it seemed that we were in lockdown mode with severe thunderstorm warnings. Growing up in Iowa, where tornados tear across the prairie like spinning tops all summer long, I was a little surprised when I first moved to Chicago to realize that we don't get many tornados here. In the suburbs—Joliet, Naperville, Woodstock—yes. But in the city proper, where we live, the tornadoes seem to be repelled either by the tall buildings or maybe by Lake Michigan. In my twenty years of living in the city, I remember only one true tornado scare.

But the storms of 2011 were often just as strong as a tornado. Blasts of winds would pound our condo windows and the trees outside. We lost so many beautiful trees. Huge, century-old oaks and maples on our block lay across streets and sidewalks like stoic, fallen soldiers. I was praying that the fragile-looking trees outside our windows would survive. After one storm, a huge branch from one of the maples fell on a car parked on the street. But the tree itself seemed that it would remain standing.

One morning, while David's brother was here visiting, I left our condo to walk ten minutes to the L. It was a little cloudy when I left, and I had grabbed my umbrella, but I wasn't aware of any storm warnings. A few minutes into my walk, I felt sprinkles on my face. I picked up my pace, hoping to make it to the L stop before it started raining harder.

I walked up Wolcott, and then to Rogers Street. I walked faster. I heard thunder. And then—*boom!*—a huge bolt of lightning struck nearby. My heart was pounding. It was about the same distance back to the condo as it was to the Howard Street L station, so I just kept walking, almost at a jog. *I can make it!* I kept thinking. But then, out of nowhere, the wind picked up, and soon I was almost blown off the sidewalk and into a fence. What seemed like hurricane-force, straight-line winds (I later found out they were around seventy mph) bent the trees so that the top leaves almost touched the sidewalk. I heard a crack to my right; an old tree was falling. I ran forward to try to avoid the falling tree. I couldn't breathe. Whether it was fear, or panic, or the sudden drop in air pressure, I felt as if I were suffocating, and a deluge was soaking me from head to foot. I didn't know what to do. I was stopped in the middle of the sidewalk. Up ahead, I saw an alley. I thought that maybe if I ducked into it, I could get away from the wind.

I staggered toward the alley. I leaned against the brick side of the building. The wind was still blowing, but I was a little bit protected. I reached for my now-soaked cell phone. I wasn't sure it would still work.

I managed to call home, and David answered. "Where are you?"

I could barely speak, I was so out of breath and panicked. "I'm in an alley, the one by the Walgreens! I'm soaked! Please come!"

When David picked me up a few minutes later, my wet clothes were hanging on my body, and my hair was plastered to my head, big drops of water dripping onto the car seat.

David took me home. I walked up the back stairs and Jim, his brother, said, "Oh, you poor thing!" I just smiled and walked into the kitchen to dry off.

Like Job and Larry Gopnik, I really wanted answers from God about why my life was turning out the way it was. I didn't get any answers. But slowly the questions settled into my soul for the long haul, and I was getting used to having them there. They felt like ballast, keeping me upright and centered as I moved from one day to the next, looking for signs of God.

13

Crossing Over

Where there is ruin, there is hope for a treasure.

—Rumi

If my suffering was a journey across and through something—*pascha*—then it was in the fall of 2011 when I started seeing the other side.

We had decided to end our international adoption quest. It was not to be. A new dream would have to develop.

For the longest time I couldn't see it. And that, I came to believe, was the worst part of suffering. If only I could see the end of the story. Then, maybe I would understand why I had to cross through the cold, deep waters of the river to get to the other side.

Although I had caught glimpses of the Ghost God—like crumbs in the children's tale of Hansel and Gretel—leading me forward, I couldn't see enough to make me feel OK about what was happening to me.

But slowly, I started trusting the breadcrumbs enough to keep going.

Although David and I had let go of our dream to adopt, we still couldn't get the idea out of our heads that a child would be in our lives. We didn't know how or when, but we didn't feel that our family was yet complete.

We had thought about adopting through the Illinois Foster Care system; then we wouldn't have to pass the severe financial inspection by the U.S. Citizenship and Immigration Services that we had to with international adoption. But we had dismissed foster care for a few reasons. First, we didn't know if we could emotionally handle caring for a child with the hopes of adopting, only to have the child returned to a biological parent who may or may not have the capacity to fully care for the child. Second, the children who were totally free for adoption (these were called "no risk" adoptions, meaning there was no risk of the biological parents getting them back), were much older—seven or above—and often had been physically, emotionally, or sexually abused. While I liked the idea of providing a safe harbor for these children, we doubted our ability to parent these troubled kids.

But we had friends who were foster parents. We observed them and decided we could at least check it out. If we felt, down the road, that it wasn't for us, we could always stop the process of getting licensed.

My whole perspective changed when I met Mary.

Mary was helping teach our Foster Care PRIDE classes. She had been a single mother to her three biological children, and then, when she was laid off from her City of Chicago job as a city planner, she had decided to get licensed to be a foster parent.

She told stories about the children she had fostered. I was in awe. One story in particular struck me. She told us about a beautiful, thirteen-year-old girl who was brought to her home. I'll call the girl "Brittany." Brittany's mother had died, and now she was a ward of the state. Mary would be her foster mother.

Mary told us about how the social worker brought this beautiful blonde, seemingly innocent little girl to her doorstep. But as soon as the social worker left, Brittany, in a defiant tone, told Mary in no uncertain terms: "I'm sexually active, and you can't stop me."

Mary was taken aback. The girl was only thirteen. But Mary remained calm.

Soon, Mary discovered that Brittany would leave the house to sell her little body to men. She was prostituting herself on street corners and in parking lots. Whenever Mary discovered that Brittany was gone, she would call the police. The police would find Brittany and bring her back to Mary.

While some parents in Mary's situation would have yelled and screamed at Brittany to stop her destructive behavior, Mary, in her infinite wisdom as a foster mother, knew better. She knew that before Brittany could stop her behavior, she needed to feel loved and valued for who she was—not for the sex that she could offer.

So every time the police brought Brittany back home, Mary would simply ask her two questions: "Are you okay?" and "Would you like something to eat?"

Then Mary would draw a bath for Brittany.

Mary's unconditional love and care for Brittany eventually started making a difference. Brittany stopped prostituting as frequently, and eventually she stopped altogether. Then Brittany graduated from high school, joined the military, and today is happily married with a daughter of her own.

Tears welled up in my eyes as I heard Mary talk about Brittany and the other troubled kids she had loved back from the darkness.

In Mary, I saw how powerful love could be. Suddenly, my fear of fostering or adopting a troubled child lessened.

Of course, I knew that if we ended up parenting a child like Brittany, or with other kinds of brokenness, it would be difficult. But I also saw the rewards.

"Isn't it really hard?" I asked Mary. Up until this point in our classes, the emphasis had been on how damaged foster children could be.

"Oh, no," said Mary. "This is my passion! Don't let these classes scare you. It is so rewarding."

I wanted to be like Mary. While being realistic, I wanted to be able to love a child to wholeness.

Even though David and I would probably foster younger children, ages newborn to five, I now knew that if we ended up with an older child who was damaged because of sexual or physical abuse or emotional neglect, I was willing to give it a try. My compassion for these children was growing. I wanted to help them.

I realized that maybe clinging to our hopes of international adoption was some kind of attempt to try to avoid what could be a difficult ride. Ethiopian children, while orphaned, more often than not had grown up in loving homes until their parents had died from AIDS or malaria. So many of these children did not suffer from attachment issues and adjusted well after they were adopted. With foster care, adopting an older child pretty much came with a guarantee that the child had suffered some severe abuse. To be honest, getting involved with the Illinois Foster Care System would be signing up to get involved with the messiness of life. It meant dealing with an imperfect system. It meant that if we were to adopt, we may be required to remain in contact with the birth family—on the whole, best for the child, but more complicated for us. And we would be dealing with the realities of how some children are treated in our society.

To be honest, international adoption seemed more sexy. There was the fun of learning about another country, of traveling overseas, of helping children affected by the AIDS crisis. Of having an airport homecoming like my sisters had when they brought their daughters home from China.

While we had legitimate reasons for wanting to adopt an Ethiopian child, I had to confess my less-altruistic reasons as well. I needed to let go of my romanticized ideas of adoption. Children needed help both abroad and here, right in my backyard. It was obvious which door was opening.

And now I could see how rewarding even this scary scenario of foster care could be, and I was beginning to envision how I could help these children who needed love.

I was also in awe of the two adult women in our foster care class who had both survived growing up in foster care. They knew what it was like, yet now they were getting licensed to foster other children. They were strong, beautiful, resilient women who had been through so much but selflessly wanted to provide homes for kids whose childhoods were just like theirs had been.

Unlike international adoption, the foster care system was welcoming us with open arms. I always felt that our condo was too small, but our foster care social worker said our spare bedroom "was huge! You could fit four kids in here!"

And when I mentioned our advancing ages, she laughed and said "What are you talking about! You're both so young!"

Like my friend Karyn says, "We don't get to choose which door God opens."

It seemed that the foster care option door was opening. It's not what I expected, but this was the door that was opening for us at this point, and we were ready to walk through it.

We finished our foster care classes in November, and I approached Advent of 2011 with hope but also a little trepidation. For my family, Christmas is a time When Bad Things Happen.

My grandmother, Mable Beattie, died of cancer right after Christmas of 1963. My other grandmother, Edna Wistrom, died on December 23, 1997. And then my mother died suddenly, unexpectedly, tragically, exactly three years later, on December 23, 2000.

Ten years after my mom died, it seemed like a cruel joke when I got a call at five in the morning from my brother, telling me that

Dad was in the ICU with a dissected aorta. A very serious condition that was life threatening.

Seriously? Ten years almost to the day of my mother's death? My dad is in the ICU?

I spent hours in that waiting room—waiting for news, waiting for doctors, waiting for my dad to turn a corner, waiting for sisters to come to relieve my night watch. And as I sat by my dad's bedside, watching the monitors, worrying at his labored breathing or his low blood-oxygen level, I realized that it wasn't overwhelming me. Unlike when my mother had died years before, when my whole world turned upside down, I had an inner calm that whispered, *God is still good. Something holy is happening here. Open your eyes, and you will see it.*

Even though I was scared shitless that my father could die, I had peace.

Now, a year later, my father had recovered and was healthy, at least for a seventy-nine-year-old. David and I both had jobs and had made considerable progress on paying off our debt and getting our finances under control.

But remembering Christmases past, during Advent of 2011 I was waiting for the other shoe to drop. What would it be? Another job loss? Another illness?

Around this time, I got an e-mail from my friend Pam. She and her husband had been fostering a baby girl, Olivia. "How are foster care classes going?" she wrote in her e-mail. "By the way, just curious, but what age and gender are you hoping to foster and possibly adopt?"

I thought her questions were a little curious. But I wrote her back:

"Hi Pam! We finished most of our foster care classes. However, we have a few more to make up in January. In the meantime, we're finishing up our paperwork. Hopefully, we'll be licensed to be foster parents by the end of January or early February. Scary, but exciting! We're not sure, but at this point we'll probably be open to fostering children 0-5 years old. We're open to either gender, but personally, I've always envisioned myself with a little girl. :)"

A few days later, Pam and I talked on the phone. She filled me in on Olivia, who was now two years old. Her biological mother was very young—it was a complicated situation. But there might be a possibility that Olivia would become available for adoption, because after a year and a half of trying to get the biological mother to comply with her "goals" for getting her child back, the social worker wasn't seeing much progress. In Illinois, typically the parents have about a year to start showing some kind of effort in getting their lives together enough to parent their child again. If they are showing little or no effort, the needs of the child become paramount, and that typically means finding a permanent placement in an adoptive home.

The state wants to avoid having the children languish in the foster care system, waiting years and years for their parents to pull themselves together and function as parents.

So, Pam asked, would we be open to having Pam mention our names to the social worker as possible foster-to-adoptive parents? She wasn't sure what the protocol was and didn't want to do anything inappropriate. But she thought she could at least mention our name to the social worker and let her take it from there.

Yes.

Yes. Yes. Yes.

But even as I said those words, I was afraid. What would happen if my dream of adoption really did come true? What then? Would I like being a parent? Could I do it? Would I be overwhelmed? After all, we were "older" parents. Would we have the energy?

I was also afraid to hope. Afraid that it *wouldn't* happen. After all our other attempts at welcoming a child into our lives, could it be as easy as this? A foster child—a girl in the age range we had always pictured—from close friends who we knew had taken excellent care of her for the past year and a half, who had helped her attach and get a solid start in life? Who had loved her and doted on her?

Our vision was to have a family. I couldn't imagine that all the picture pieces could fit together so perfectly. I was imagining adopting Olivia and having visits with "Aunt Pam and Uncle Jonathan," the foster parents who had given her a solid start in life. I imagined us all being part of a big family who had come together to give this little girl a forever family while still helping her remain in contact with her biological mother.

Was this too much to hope for, God? Would you give me this kind of abundance? Did I deserve it?

I tried to balance the hope and excitement with my fear of becoming a parent, and the fear that my vision would fall apart, that Olivia would return to her biological mother, or that another adoptive family would be chosen. I had to live in this tension.

On December 23, on the eleventh anniversary of my mother's death, during Advent, when we were waiting for the Christ child and Old Saint Pat's was decked out in its holiday finest, I got an e-mail from Pam:

"I just talked with Ms. L, the supervisor of Olivia's case, this morning in response to this e-mail below that I had sent her early in December telling her about you and David and suggesting that it might be a good idea for Olivia to be adopted by a couple we know, to make her transition easier. She said she thought it was a great suggestion and said that the next step is to get a clinical staffing scheduled for Olivia's case where the entire team can talk about and plan the next steps for her."

I got chills as I read the e-mail. I was excited, afraid, hopeful, yet cautious.

As we waited for the Christ child to come, and as my thoughts were focused on my own mother, I was waiting to see what would happen with Olivia. If she would be our child.

We were going to see Olivia on New Year's Day. We had met her briefly six months before. But that was long before we knew it was possible we might adopt her.

It still was far from a sure thing. Many pieces had to fall into place. But David and I would be going to Pam and John's house for a New Year's Day party, and we'd see Olivia.

It's very odd to go to a party and know you'll see the little two-year-old girl who may—or may not—become your daughter.

Eventually. Possibly. Probably not. But maybe.

What was I supposed to feel? Was I supposed to hope that I would "connect" with her at some level? What if I didn't? Or what if I *did*?! What if I walked into John and Pam's house and saw Olivia and had an immediate reaction that she was supposed to be my daughter? And then it didn't happen?

Adoption is strange that way. I've heard that some adoptive parents don't immediately attach to their adoptive children. Others know immediately—upon seeing a photo—that this particular child is "theirs."

So I knew that I may not be immediately drawn to Olivia. And to top it all off, we weren't even sure that I should let myself feel anything, with things so much up in the air. There was a part of me that I had to protect because there was a good chance this would go nowhere and we'd still be childless a year from now.

So I went to John and Pam's party with butterflies in my stomach, anxious about what I would feel when I got there. Driving to Oak Park, I prayed silently, *God, help me to be open, knowing that whatever happens, I will remember that this story has already ended with so much resurrection, I can't even begin to fathom it.*

When we arrived, Olivia came running out of the kitchen in a bright pink outfit with a frilly skirt, her dark curls framing her round face. "HI!" she yelled, announcing her presence to everyone in the room, making the adults surrounding her chuckle.

She wiggled her butt in a little dance and then dropped to the floor to show off her "break dance" moves that her foster brother had taught her.

I was drawn to this little pink bundle of energy. The moment I saw her, I felt a crack in my heart and a flutter in my stomach. I knew I could welcome this child into our lives.

Later, David and I awkwardly sat with her as she ate strawberries, one after another, at the dining room table, the juice dripping off her chin as she grinned at us. She looked at us with her sweet face, not knowing whether we were friends or foes. I wondered, *Does she like us? What is she thinking?* But by the end of the night, I think we had won her over.

Later, she dragged me downstairs to the family room, her chubby brown hand in mine as we navigated the basement stairs. Downstairs there was so much to do! So much to see!

Olivia ran full speed ahead for a shelf of puzzles. We pulled one from the shelf, and she followed me to the table, where we could spread out the pieces. She kept looking up at me: *Who are you? What are you doing down here with me?*

I was thinking the same thing.

David sat down with us, and the three of us put together a puzzle of the United States. The three of us. Together. Was this our future?

I didn't know. It would take months before we would know if she would be available for adoption and if DCFS would choose us as her foster-to-adopt parents.

I had to live in this in-between time of not knowing. Of it all being a mystery, of searching for Ghost God. This was a place I knew well. I was in the middle of the cold, deep river, and I felt the slippery rocks beneath my feet. I could smell the fresh water and maybe even whiffs of wet mud from the opposite side. I was catching glimpses of land, here with this tiny, grinning two-year-old. I thought maybe I felt a bit of hope, as she looked at me with her chestnut eyes.

Something was happening. I didn't know what it was yet, but I would keep putting my feet on the slippery rocks, the water rushing around my ankles, moving forward until I reached the other shore.

Epilogue

"Where is my home?"

She looked at me, paused a minute, and then went back to stuffing pasta into her mouth, the tiny spoon clutched in her chubby three-year-old hand.

"Your home is here," I answered. "Your bed is in there. You belong here." I pointed into her bedroom just off the kitchen.

"Oh," she whispered.

Olivia had been with us for about a month. The month had been a blur of adjusting, getting settled, finding places for her toys and clothes in our small condo, deciding where she would go to daycare, and trying to get her to sleep at night, which she often refused to do, tossing and turning in her toddler bed for hours.

We didn't know what we were doing. She didn't know why she was here.

We were all trying to keep our heads above water.

Months earlier, we had been told that adopting Olivia was not an option. The agency said that other families were waiting—other families who had been licensed for a while. We were still in the midst of taking foster care classes. By the time we were finished, Olivia would have already been placed in an adoptive home.

We had moved on. Deep down, I had started thinking that maybe, just maybe, it was time to let this dream of adoption go, the way I had let go of other dreams. I was starting to imagine our life without a child. I knew our life was abundant, even though we would always feel a hole right in the place where a child was supposed to be.

But I had heard Father Foley, a priest at my church, say that when there is a hole in our lives, it's an opportunity for God to fill it with holiness. That if we have open hands and hearts, the holiness of God might touch us. I was hanging on to that hope.

Then, one afternoon in June, I received a phone call. An official voice from the agency posed this question: "I'm calling you to see if you'd consider being foster-to-adoptive parents to Olivia Thompson?" (name changed).

After pursuing three other potential adoptive homes for Olivia—placements that had fallen through for various reasons—the agency was calling us.

"I have to talk to my husband," I said, my hands shaking. "When do you need an answer?"

"Within the next few days," he said.

⋮

——————

There's always danger in saying yes. After awhile, a dream becomes abstract and idealized. Saying yes lassoes it and pulls that dream down to earth, where things are messy and uncertain and hard and you question yourself when things go wrong.

About a month after Olivia moved in, as I was rocking her to sleep, she cried, her little body buckling against mine. She arched her back and stiffened her legs, trying to get away from my embrace. Since arriving, she had resisted being cuddled or rocked. She pushed me away as I tried to wrap my arms around her.

This went on for thirty minutes, but finally she gave up and fell back onto my chest, her head resting just under my chin. I felt her curls on my face.

Neither of us wanted it to be this way. This was her third home. This wasn't how it was supposed to be. She was meant to be born into a family who loved her and could care for her. She didn't deserve to be taken from her home and put into State protection because her teenage parents couldn't provide for her or keep her safe.

It wasn't supposed to be this way. David and I were supposed to have been parents long ago—when we were younger and had more energy. Not after years of riding the emotional roller coaster of adoption to the point of exhaustion.

But here we both were, for better or for worse.

She whimpered in my arms. She was tired of struggling to get away from me. I was bone tired from the stress of parenthood and trying to get her to sleep.

In the dark bedroom, we both cried. Her brown skin pressed against mine. We cried together in that rocking chair, but in the darkness I could feel God's holiness filling up the empty places.

"You are home," I whispered through my tears, into her dark, curly hair. "You are home."

Endnotes

1. Richard Rohr, *Everything Belongs: The Gift of Contemplative Prayer*, Revised ed. (Chestnut Ridge, NY : Crossroad, 2003), 43.

2. Scot McNight, *The Real Mary: Why Evangelical Christians Can Embrace the Mother of Jesus* (Orleans, MA: Paraclete Press, 2007), 8–9.

3. Henri Nouwen, *Clowning in Rome: Reflections on Solitude, Celibacy, Prayer, and Contemplation* (New York: Doubleday, 1979), 44.

4. http://www.huffingtonpost.com/eric-simpson/ what-it-means-to-be-poor-_b_788700.html

5. http://www.scientificamerican.com/ article.cfm?id=how-wealth-reduces-compassion. Accessed September 3, 2012.

6. David L. Fleming, *Draw Me Into Your Friendship: The Spiritual Exercises, A Literal Translation & A Contemporary Reading* (St. Louis: The Institute of Jesuit Sources, 1996), 113.

7. Ibid., 113, 115.

8. http://www.gotquestions.org/narrative-theology.html

Acknowledgements

"Set your life on fire. Seek those who fan your flames," wrote the poet Rumi. When Vinita Hampton Wright and Joe Durepos approached me about the possibility of writing for Loyola Press, they fanned the flames, and I never would have finished this book without their encouragement. Every time I sent a chapter to Vinita, I waited nervously for her response. And each time I received an email in response, it was warm, kind, and encouraging. She helped me believe that I could actually finish writing a book, which at times felt like running a marathon. She was my cheering section, and her emails were just what I needed to start the next chapter and keep going. Thank you for believing in me.

Others who have fanned the flames are Amy Wolgemuth Bordoni and Angela Doll Carlson, who throughout the years have read my work in our little writers group and traveled with me to various writing conferences. The three of us have held on to dreams of writing things that would make a difference in the world—and we have shared our passion for books and words. Amy and Angela are true kindred spirits and writing companions on this journey.

My father, Bob Beattie, instilled in me a love for literature and reading. I remember sitting on my parents' bed as a child while my dad read from a book of poetry. These were the first memories of hearing beautiful words, and I thank my dad for giving me this love for words. I also want to thank the rest of my family for allowing me to write about our family and for always being there for me.

It is obvious throughout this book that the Beloved Community at Old Saint Pat's was integral to the writing of this book. I want to thank the entire Beloved Community, but especially Terry Nelson-Johnson who, through his teaching and storytelling, showed me a whole new way to experience my faith. Laura Field, my spiritual director; Karen Skalitzky, my RCIA sponsor; Alexis Michael and my other RCIA tablemates; and the St. Ignatius Retreat group of 2011.

Finally, to David, who endured many lonely Saturdays by himself while I was writing at a table in Starbucks, who put up with my self-doubts and insecurities, who served as my first reader and editor, and who offered invaluable feedback and ideas throughout the entire process of writing this book. You make my life rich.

About the Author

Karen Beattie has been a writer for more than 20 years and has been published in several publications including *Christianity Today* and *Midwest Living*. She recently became a Catholic, and she and her husband attend Old St. Patrick's in Chicago, Illinois.

Continue the Conversation

If you enjoyed this book, then connect with Loyola Press to continue the conversation, engage with other readers, and find out about new and upcoming books from your favorite spiritual writers.

Visit us at **www.LoyolaPress.com** to create an account and register for our newsletters.

Or you can just click on the code to the right with your smartphone to sign up.

Connect with us on the following:

Facebook
facebook.com/loyolapress

Twitter
twitter.com/loyolapress

You Tube
youtube.com/loyolapress